Community Life

ESL

ACCESSTRUTH

Community Life ESL

First Edition

Copyright © 2020 AccessTruth

ISBN: 978-0-6484151-9-0

Author: Grace Hillier
Illustrator: Charlene Gilmour

Published by AccessTruth
PO Box 8087
Baulkham Hills NSW 2153
Australia

Email: info@accesstruth.com
Web: accesstruth.com

Eighty Lessons for Teaching Community-Based English

Preface

"An hour or two in class each week is not enough for my students to learn English. What should I do?" is a question every English teacher has asked themselves. This book poses a solution. What if the hour of English *teaching* turned into English *consulting*; modelling to students how to learn English in their own communities outside the classroom?

Community Life ESL has been adapted from Becoming Equipped to Communicate (BEC), a culture and language program which was developed to equip people to communicate fluently in cross-cultural situations.

Community Life ESL is designed to equip students to develop deep relationships in the community. Upon completion of this program, students will have developed numerous relationships in their new community as a normal part of their process of learning. In this sense, Community Life ESL is not just a language learning program, it is a program in which students will learn to function in their new community — to speak, to listen, to interact in natural ways and to take part in people's lives.

Contents

Level 3: Relating through Sharing Life Stories

Understanding a Story

Retelling a Story

Telling Your Own Story

Level 4: Relating through Worldview Conversations

Extra Term of Lessons:

Appendix

Why This Program?

Community Life ESL is designed for students who want to spend time with local people, learning through personal interaction and involvement in community life - not for those who are engaged only in formal tutoring or classroom sessions.

In the Weekly Homework Activities for instance, students will need to spend time with a growing number of local people as they participate in community life. Investing time in getting to know people from the outset is a foundational part of this program. Community Life ESL is designed to help students grow toward achieving a healthy and sustainable level of community engagement by the time they reach the end of the program. This can be challenging at the beginning, but well worth it.

Below are the overall learning principles that have shaped this program - try to make a habit of referring to them often.

Community Life ESL Key Learning Principles

» Relationship: Learning means getting to know people, taking place in the context of relationships - as your students spend time interacting with people.

» Culture: Learning means getting exposure to real life; to significant amounts of culture and language as they happen naturally.

» Comprehension: Your students will learn language through trying to understand, and comprehension will come before speaking ability.

» Communication: Your students will learn more, and better, if they are really trying to communicate something to someone in order to get a response.

» Proficiency: 'Proficiency' is what your students are able to do with language and how they are able to function in activities in the community.

Teaching Philosophy

We in the AccessTruth team are excited that many people (who once lived in unreached people groups with no access to the Good News of Jesus) have moved to the Western world. We see teaching English as a practical way to not only bridge the language barrier, but also to build relationships with these people in the hope that they may one day hear the Gospel.

Community Life ESL empowers churches to carry out English teaching effectively. This program was designed to fill a need for hands-on, relationship-centered learning. Experience has shown that learning takes place best within community, so all activities in Community Life ESL are designed to equip students to foster deep relationships and involvement in their community. So, although we are glad for anyone to utilize Community Life ESL in the classroom, we love when community involvement is used as the most fundamental instrument of the learning process.

Get Ready

Know your students

Equipping students to become part of a new community through learning culture and language is a long but rewarding process. As you prepare for this multi-year journey, learn everything you can about your students.

As your students begin to get settled in their new community, they will feel overwhelmed by all there is to learn about how to relate to others. They can't take it all in at once! Remind students how important it is to invest time and energy into a few relationships at the beginning with people in the community like neighbors, work colleagues and children's teachers.

Encourage your students to spend as much time as possible where people usually spend most of their time, like shopping centers or parks, and to become familiar with these places.

Plan

Your students will need to create a broad plan for themselves that allows them to spend as much time as possible learning to communicate, while maintaining a healthy family life. The more consistent, concentrated and intensive they are, and the more time and energy they invest in their learning, the quicker their ability to communicate will grow.

Encourage the students to try to be creative and flexible and to include their family, household activities or their workplace environment as their learning setting. They can visit local homes with their family, cook or shop with a friend, listen to class recordings while doing laundry, and learn the 'local way' of doing things.

Preparing Lessons

This book contains everything you will need to teach lessons, including pictures and Homework templates. You will need to procure your own props for lessons however, as real objects are invaluable when teaching new vocabulary. Pictures for Level 1 activities are still in development, so you will also need to find your own pictures for this level for the time being.

When preparing for a lesson in Level 2, you will need to print enough copies of the pictures for each student to have their own set, as well as the Homework templates specified in the lesson.

Homework

Each week students will be given Homework that will help them participate in the community. They will need to gradually fit in with the life and routines of their new community, so encourage them to relax and be flexible. It will take them some time to establish a routine for their lives that includes regular and sustainable community involvement. You will need to give students ideas for community activities which they can participate in each week as part of their Homework in Level 1. Some ideas are provided for you on the Community Activity Template in the Appendix. These activities will help familiarize students with the routines and activities that they will undertake in Level 2.

Learning in community

Remind your students to meet regularly with people in their community. Finding people who have the time and are willing to meet with them may be one of their biggest challenges.

Their learning will also include informal times of being a part of their new community, taking part in community life and events. Remind your students that things might not work out exactly as they planned. But they DO need a plan to begin with. Because of the dynamic nature of community life, they will need to constantly adjust their schedules as they find different people to spend time with and new community activities in which to take part.

It can be easier for students if their schedules include a lot of planned, routine activities that are a regular part of life. Relying only on spontaneous activities or meetings with community members outside of their regular English classes will not give them enough time immersed in the language and culture during this critical learning time.

Church relationships

Many churches have programs where people volunteer as English helpers in class. While this is important, it is also helpful to have people volunteer to spend time with students outside of class, helping them with the Homework Activities, practicing conversation and inviting them to join in community and church activities.

Absolute beginners

It is important that the students have a designated language helper who speaks both their langauge and English (ideally a friend of theirs) who can assist them with Homework Activities during the week. For absolute beginners, it is best if their helper is also invited along to English class.

For absolute beginners, you will need to use your discretion with Homework Activities. In this case, Homework will only be possible if they have a designated language helper who can explain the Homework to them. If this is not possible, then disregard Homework Activities for Level 1.

TPR

Total Physical Response (TPR) is a language teaching method that involves learning language with movement. It is used extensively in each lesson throughout the first level of Community Life ESL. Teachers give commands to students to perform specific actions and students listen and respond with the actions.

Listening and responding allows students to quickly recognize meaning and is an effective way for absolute beginners to learn vocabulary. It is actually the way that we all learned to speak as children; first we listened to our parents and responded without any pressure to speak.

Go at the students' pace

Best teaching practice is to go at the students' pace. If the students need revision, then take the time to revise past lessons. It's ok to stop in the middle of a lesson and pick it up the next week if the students need more practice.

Remember, learning English can be fun! Enjoy your students and this opportunity to invest in their lives.

Placement Test

Before beginning English class, it is best practice to test the students first. Use the Placement Test to determine which level to place students in, especially if you are holding classes for different levels. If you can only hold one class, then you will need to begin at the lowest student's level.

Review

At the beginning of each lesson there is time set aside for Review. Use this time to check students' Homework. Ask about how their community activities went and if they were able to observe any common routines. Did they run into any challenges? Did they meet any new people? They should also have transcribed (written down) their recordings from the previous lesson. Check these for accuracy (if you have English helpers, they can assist you with this).

Recordings

At the beginning of each lesson, explain to the students that they will be using their phones to make recordings. They will record what you say and then listen to this during the week as part of their Homework. The more they practice their English, the more they will learn! The steps below will help students to get the most out of their recordings:

1. Have students record an example of the learned content in the lesson (you could also generate the recordings for your students before class and pass it on to them. Sometimes classrooms can be too noisy to take recordings, and this will also save time in class).

2. Have students transcribe the whole recording.

3. Have students practice repeating their recordings, sentence by sentence, as they actively point to their pictures.

4. Finally, have students try repeating the lesson content along with the recording as they actively point to their pictures. The goal is for them to do this without needing to pause the recording.

5. Have students bring their transcriptions to class where you and other English speakers can check for accuracy.

Note: If your students are illiterate then they will not be able to transcribe the recordings, so make this is an optional step for those who can read and write.

The Four Levels of Community Life ESL

The overall proficiency goal of the program is Capable High (this roughly corresponds to 6.5 - 8.0 in IELTS, Advanced-high in ACTFL and 79-114 in TEOFL). This is a realistic goal if the students complete all 80 lessons over 2 years and seriously commit to practicing their language skills outside the classroom. This is described as "market-level" proficiency, meaning once completed, students will be able to participate in the community in natural ways. Once students reach this level it will be possible for them to attend a Bible Study and actively engage with a church community.

This book contains lessons that help students progress through four levels of language as they grow their relationships with others in the community. Ideally, they will be learning language full time, but we realize that is not possible for all students as many will have jobs and other commitments.

Level 1: Relating through the common and familiar

During **Level 1** students will learn to relate to others by learning to recognize the most common words, familiar phrases, simple sentence patterns and questions that local people use every day.

Level 2: Relating through daily routines

During **Level 2** students will relate to others by recognizing and creating sentences in English, asking and answering simple questions, talking about what is becoming familiar to them and everyday activities in the community. They will be able to understand and use sentences rather than just words and phrases.

Level 3: Relating through sharing life stories

During **Level 3** students will relate to others through explaining, comparing and describing things that already happened, are happening or will happen later. At this level they will be able to understand and speak in paragraphs instead of just single sentences. They will be able to handle situations where something unexpected occurs and they will talk about their own and other's life experiences.

Level 4: Relating through worldview conversation

Level 4 is the final level, during which students will learn to understand and talk about the beliefs that motivate the behavior of both themselves and others. They will be able to understand the opinions of others as well as support their own opinions. They will also talk about events and ideas that are potential but haven't happened yet. They will be able to connect paragraphs together to form long texts in their conversations.

Comparison of Proficiency Levels

IELTS	0.0 - 4.0		4.0 - 4.5	5.0 - 6.0	6.5 - 8.0	8.5 - 9.0
BEC	Basic Low/mid/high	Progressing Low/mid/high	Capable-low	Capable-mid	Capable-high	Proficient
ACTFL	Novice Low/mid/high	Intermediate Low/mid/high	Advanced-low	Advanced-mid	Advanced-high	Superior
TOEFL	0 - 31		31-34	35-59	79-114	115-120

Self-rating Checklist

	Description	Self-rating Checklist
Level 1	By the end of Level 1 I am... Able to ask questions and make simple statements based on memorized sentences. Understand conversation fragments and simple commands. Able to deal with simple topics of daily need though I speak mostly in short, direct sentences. I can say some longer phrases and sentences if given time to think about them first. Though I still make frequent errors in pronunciation and word use, and frequently ask speakers to slow down or repeat, I can communicate with close acquaintances (e.g., host family or co-workers). Behave considerately in dealing with host country nationals. Understand some nonverbal cues.	• I can initiate and close conversations appropriately. • I understand and can make simple statements about family, animals, emotions, weather, daily activities, time, date, and day of the week. • I understand some words when the context helps explain them, e.g., the grocery store or the doctor's office. • My vocabulary includes names of basic concepts: days, months, numbers, articles of clothing, body parts, and family relationships. • I can use at least one hundred nouns and verbs in appropriate contexts. • I still find it difficult to understand native speakers (in spite of my growing vocabulary).
Level 2	By the end of Level 2 I am... Able to participate in conversations about most survival needs, limited social conventions, and other topics. Get the gist of most conversations on familiar topics. Able to discuss topics beyond basic survival, such as personal history and leisure time activities. Though I speak mostly in short, discrete sentences, I show occasional bursts of spontaneity. Can use most question forms, basic tenses, pronouns, and verb inflections, though I still speak with many errors. Can be understood by native speakers used to speaking with foreigners. By repeating things, I can frequently be understood by the general public. In dealing with host country citizens, I'm able to get along in familiar survival situations and with native speakers accustomed to foreigners.	• I can introduce myself or someone else in some detail. • I can buy my basic foodstuffs, rent a hotel room, visit the doctor and do housework. • I can join in local activities, like attend a sports game and make a local meal. • I can talk about favorite pastimes or sports. • I can join in leisure activities, like go on a bush walk, go to the beach or play a local game. • I can go to places where people gather in the community, like church, the library or the movies. • I can carry on more complicated conversations with native speakers who are used to dealing with foreigners. • I find myself thinking some words and sentences in my new language and offering them spontaneously.

Level 3	By the end of Level 3 I am... Able to handle most work requirements and conversations on technical or work-related topics of interest. Able to express facts, give instructions, describe, report, and talk about current, past, and future activities. Often I am able to speak fluently and easily, though occasionally I must pause to think of a word. I still make some grammatical errors.	• I can understand a story and retell it. • I can compare and contrast events. • I can deal with unexpected and unusual situations. • I can talk with ease about my past, my current activities, and what I hope to do in the future. • I generally speak easily and fluently with only minor pauses.
Level 4	By the end of Level 4 I am... Able to converse on most practical, social, and professional topics. Able to deal with unfamiliar topics, provide explanations, resolve problems, describe in detail, offer supported opinions, and hypothesize. I am able to talk about simple abstract ideas. I rarely have to grope for a word. My control of grammar is good and errors almost never seem to bother the native speaker. Able to participate appropriately in most social and work situations. In dealing with native speakers, I am able to understand common rules of etiquette, taboos and sensitivities, and handle routine social situations when dealing with people accustomed to foreigners.	• I can make culturally acceptable requests, accept or refuse invitations, apologize, and follow social rules for visiting. • I can support my opinions in a discussion or argument. • I understand what is considered shameful and praiseworthy behaviour. • I understand common roles and responsibilities in society and what is considered as successful and unsuccessful. • I can talk about government, family life and beliefs about the spiritual world. • I can carry out most work assignments in the target language. • I can handle routine social situations with ease. • I can participate effectively in most general discussions involving native speakers. • I can deal with an unexpected problem or a social blunder. I seldom have to ask speakers to repeat or explain. • I can speak at a normal rate of speed, without groping for words or trying to avoid complex grammatical structures.

Sample Scope and Sequence: Level 1 and 2

This scope and sequence illustrates the delivery of Community Life ESL in a classroom setting. This course spans 2 years, totaling 80 classroom hours.

Term 1	Week 1	Week 2	Week 3	Week 4	Week 5	Week 6	Week 7	Week 8	Week 9	Week 10
Level 1- Learning Common Words and Phrases (10 classroom hours)	This unit helps students to acquire, through understanding first, a broad vocabulary foundation that should apply in all of their relationships with others in the community. They will do this by experiencing the most common activities and by learning to understand the most common words and phrases that people use all the time in those activities. Students should not be required to speak in this unit.									

Term 2	Week 1	Week 2	Week 3	Week 4	Week 5	Week 6	Week 7	Week 8	Week 9	Week 10
Level 1- Learning Common Words and Phrases Cont. (10 classroom hours)	In this unit, students begin to incorporate speaking with their listening and acting activities. This will enable the students to move from just listening and acting to actually repeating and rephrasing those small pieces of language now that they can understand them well. They will revise simple words and phrases that they learned previously and will gradually begin speaking while they listen and act.									

Term 3	Week 1	Week 2	Week 3	Week 4	Week 5	Week 6	Week 7	Week 8	Week 9	Week 10
Level 1- Learning Common Words and Phrases Cont. (10 classroom hours)	*As above									

Term 4	Week 1	Week 2	Week 3	Week 4	Week 5	Week 6	Week 7	Week 8	Week 9	Week 10
Level 2- Relating through Daily Routines (10 classroom hours)	This unit enables students to understand and speak in whole sentences. They will also learn to understand and ask questions about what they are learning. They will focus on understanding descriptions of daily routines and activities with the help of community members. They will learn to understand appropriate questions regarding these activities, describing these daily routines and processes for themselves, and asking their own questions in turn.									

Term 1	Week 1	Week 2	Week 3	Week 4	Week 5	Week 6	Week 7	Week 8	Week 9	Week 10
Level 2- Relating through Daily Routines Cont. (10 classroom hours)	*As above									

Term 2	Week 1	Week 2	Week 3	Week 4	Week 5	Week 6	Week 7	Week 8	Week 9	Week 10
Level 2- Relating through Daily Routines (10 classroom hours)	*As above									

Sample Scope and Sequence: Level 3 and 4

This scope and sequence illustrates the delivery of Community Life ESL in a classroom setting. This course spans 2 years, a total of 80 classroom hours (the extra 10 lessons in Level 4 are optional).

Term 3	Week 1	Week 2	Week 3	Week 4	Week 5	Week 6	Week 7	Week 8	Week 9	Week 10
Level 3- Relating through Sharing Life Stories (10 classroom hours	In this unit, students relate to others through explaining, comparing, and describing things that already happened, are happening or will happen later. At this level they will be able to understand and speak in paragraphs instead of just single sentences. They will learn to handle situations in which something unexpected occurs and talk about their own life experience as well as that of others.									

Term 4	Week 1	Week 2	Week 3	Week 4	Week 5	Week 6	Week 7	Week 8	Week 9	Week 10
Level 4- Relating through Worldview Conversation (10 classroom hours)	In this unit, students complete the final level of culture and language learning, during which they learn to understand and talk about the beliefs that motivate both their behavior and that of those with whom they are building relationships. They will learn to understand other opinions as well as support their own opinions. They will begin to talk about events and ideas that are potential but haven't happened yet. They will learn to connect paragraphs together to form long texts in their conversation. They will begin to talk about the bigger issues in the world and find ways to talk about concepts that are new to them.									

Extra Term (Optional)	Week 1	Week 2	Week 3	Week 4	Week 5	Week 6	Week 7	Week 8	Week 9	Week 10
Level 4- Relating through Worldview Conversation Cont. (10 classroom hours)	*As above This unit is an optional part of the program that can be used for self-study or one on one classes with Advanced students. A church could be encouraged to start a volunteer program for people to spend time with higher level students going through this unit as they have deep conversations about worldview and culture.									

Placement Test

Administer this short test to determine which level students should be placed in (either Levels 1 and 2, or Levels 3 and 4). The test should be done one-on-one and should take no more than ten to fifteen minutes with each student. It focuses on the student's level of comprehension and speaking, rather than their reading and writing proficiency.

The questions get progressively more difficult, so stop whenever you feel the student has reached the limit of their ability.

Level 1 and 2 (Beginner) - Able to complete up to question 4.

Level 3 and 4 (Intermediate) - Able to go beyond question 4.

You will need

- A page with pictures of 10 common objects (common animals, fruits and vegetables, numbers, etc.)

- A page with pictures of 10 common objects (colours, common household objects, vehicles, etc.)

1. Casual opening conversation:

    Hello, how are you today?

    (Continue with a short conversation as you are able)

    We are going to do a short test to see which English class will be the best one for you to join.

    Are you ready to begin?

    ☐ ABLE TO RESPOND TO MOST QUESTIONS WITH EASE

2. Listen and point:

    Show the student a page with pictures of ten common objects (common animals, fruits and vegetables, numbers, etc.).

    Say to the student: *Point to the (object).*

    Have the student listen and point to each object on the page as you ask them to point to each one.

    You should always say the name of the object in a simple sentence rather than on its own, e.g., *Where is the (object)? Show me the (object).*

    You can repeat this exercise with different picture pages.

    ☐ ABLE TO NAME MOST OBJECTS WITH EASE

3. Point and Name:

    Show the student a page with pictures of ten common objects (colors, common household objects, vehicles, etc.)

    Point to each object and say to the person: *What is this?*

    Have them name as many of the objects as they can.

    You can repeat this exercise with different picture pages.

    ☐ ABLE TO NAME MOST OBJECTS WITH EASE

4. Simple questions:

    Ask the student some simple questions to allow them to demonstrate their level of comprehension and speaking.

    What is your name? _____

    Where do you live? _____

    How many children do you have? _____

    How long have you been in this country? _____

    What is your job? _____

    Where do you work? _____

    What hobbies do you have? _____

    What do you enjoy doing on the weekend? _____

    Where would you like to travel? _____

    Extra question/s_____

    ☐ ABLE TO RESPOND TO MOST QUESTIONS WITH EASE

5. Comprehension exercise:

Give the student the following story printed out. You should read the story out loud, and they can follow along reading it if they are able.

Verbally ask them the questions about the story, and if they are able, they can read the questions as well. Have them answer the questions verbally.

Bill has a young son named Sam. Sam loves to go to the park. The park is not far from their house. Sam and Bill play with a ball at the park. Bill kicks the ball, and Sam chases it. Sam is a fast runner. He kicks the ball back to Bill. Bill and Sam enjoy spending time together. Bill loves his son.

1. Who is Sam?

2. Where does Sam love to go?

3. What do Sam and Bill do at the park?

4. Where is the park?

5. How does Bill feel about Sam?

☐ ABLE TO RESPOND TO MOST QUESTIONS WITH EASE

Recommended Starting Level: _____

Able to complete up to question 4= Recommended Starting Level 1

Able to go beyond question 4= Recommended Starting Level 3

Weekly Review

☐   Listen to your recordings for the lesson (for Levels 1 and 2 you can also try pointing to the correct pictures/performing the correct action/routine).

☐   As you listen, try repeating what you hear.

☐   Write down what you hear and ask a friend who speaks English if there are any words you don't understand. Remember to bring this to class with you for the next lesson!

The End Goal

Community Life ESL is designed to help students become proficient in English. Only then will they be able to understand a Gospel message presented to them in English. That's why you won't see any Bible stories in Community Life ESL, with learning language being the primary purpose of the lessons. Of course you want your students to understand the Gospel; that's the end goal, after all, and so we at AccessTruth developed *His Story: The Rescue*. It is an overview of the Bible message in easy English and a great follow-on resource for students who have learnt English and are ready to converse using Biblical concepts and terminology.

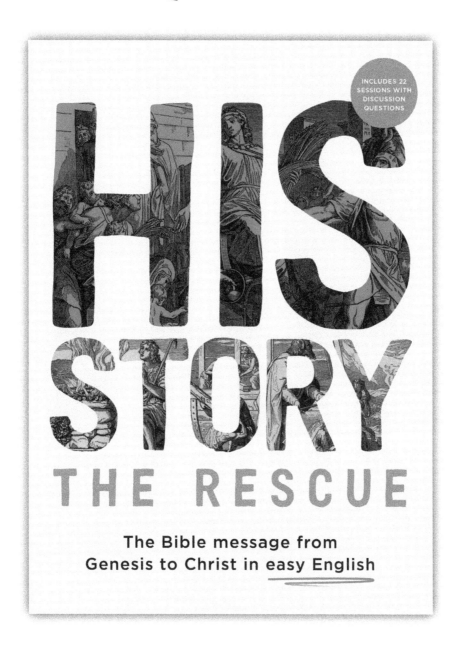

LEVEL 1 - BEGINNER

Introduction to English Class

You will need

- Introduction to English Class Paper (see Appendix- if possible, try to have the paper translated into the students' languages)
- Smartphone

Note: Before commencing teaching, make sure you have administered the Placement Test with each student. This can be administered by English speakers in class if you have any assisting you, otherwise you will need to organize to meet with each student individually.

For the first 10 lessons the students should be focusing on listening and responding with actions. Don't expect them to always respond with speaking yet, unless you are teaching them survival phrases or greetings that will be helpful for them to memorize.

Introduction

1. Introduce yourself as the teacher and write your name on the board, i.e. "Hello, my name is... and I am your teacher".

2. Go around the room and (if the students are able) have them introduce themselves, "i.e. "Hello, my name is..." Write their names on the board (10 min).

Practice

3. Model a greeting and leave-taking scenario with an English speaker, i.e. "Nice to meet you. My name is..." and "Goodbye, see you later."

4. Pair the students with an English speaker and have them role-play greeting and leave-taking scenarios with each other (10 min).

5. Give out the Introduction to English Class Paper. Go through the paper with the class so the students are familiar with the goals and expectations of the program (10 min).

   This will work best if you have someone do this who can speak the students' languages. If not, try to have the paper translated into the students' languages and just give it to them to read.

Assessment

6. If you haven't already, assess the students individually using the Placement Test (15 min).

 REPEAT THE GREETING AND LEAVE TAKING SCENARIO AGAIN AND THIS TIME HAVE STUDENTS RECORD IT ON THEIR PHONES (5 MIN).

Greeting and Leave-Taking Recording

Person 1: "Hi my name is Jacob."

Person 2: "Nice to meet you Jacob, my name is George" (shake hands).

Person 1: "It was nice meeting you George. See you later."

Person 2: "Goodbye, see you next week!", etc.

Give Homework

 Task students with finding a language helper who can assist them with their Homework for English class each week. Ideally this would be a friend who speaks both their language and English. They should show the Introduction to English Class Paper to them.

People

You will need
- Pictures of people
- Weekly Review Template (see Appendix)
- Community Activity Template (see Appendix)
- Smartphone

Review

Recap last week's lesson and check students' homework activities (10 min).

Vocabulary: baby, child, teenager, woman, man, old woman, old man, etc.

1. Show the students several pictures of people. Starting with two pictures, teach the vocabulary in the context of a sentence as you point to the picture, such as "Point to the man" or "Point to the woman." Do this several times.

2. Encourage the students to try pointing to the correct picture as you say, "Point to the woman" or "Point to the man."

3. Once the students succeed in pointing correctly to the pictures several times, add a third, then a fourth, and so on until they have learned ten to twenty new words. Go through the items randomly and unpredictably to maximize their learning (15 mins).

   Remember, you are talking, the students are just listening.

Vocabulary: I, you, he, she, it, we, they

4. Introduce vocabulary for personal pronouns. Point to pictures of people and use the pronouns in a sentence, such as "He is a man" and "She is a woman."

5. Encourage the students to point to the correct picture as you say, "She is a woman" and "He is a man."

6. Once the students succeed in pointing correctly to the pictures several times, add a third, then a fourth, and so on (15 mins).

Practice

7. Using vocabulary learnt so far, have the students point at all the others in the class that the sentence applies to, such as "Point to a man" and the students point to each man in the class. As they point, affirm what they say, such as "Yes, he is a man."

 REPEAT THE NEW VOCABULARY FOR PEOPLE AND PRONOUNS IN SENTENCES AND THIS TIME HAVE THE STUDENTS RECORD IT ON THEIR PHONES (5 MIN).

People Recording

Teacher: "Point to the man."

Student: Points to the picture of the man.

Teacher: "She is a woman."

Student: Points to the picture of the woman.

Give Homework

Review

Give the students the Weekly Review Template and a copy of the pictures used in the lesson. Tell them to listen to their recordings and practice pointing to the correct pictures during the week. They should transcribe the recordings and try repeating what they hear. Remind them to bring the transcriptions to class for the next lesson for you to check for accuracy.

Community Activity

Give the students the Community Activity Template. Encourage them to observe a common activity in the community during the week.

Note: Remind the students to ask lots of questions and take photos as they observe the activity. In Level 2 they will use this when they have to do the routines themselves.

*There is a list of suggested activities on the back of the template to give them some ideas of things they can observe in the community.

Animals

You will need
- Pictures of people and animals
- Weekly Review Template
- Community Activity Template
- Smartphone

Review

Recap last week's lesson and check students' homework activities (10 min).

Vocabulary: monkey, snake, tiger, cat, kangaroo, etc.

1. Show the students several pictures of animals. Starting with two pictures, teach the vocabulary in the context of a sentence as you point to the picture, such as "Point to the snake" or "Point to the tiger." Do this several times.

2. Encourage the students to try pointing to the correct picture as you say, "Point to the snake" or "Point to the tiger."

3. Once the students succeed in pointing correctly to the pictures several times, add a third, then a fourth, and so on until they have learned ten to twenty new words. Go through the items randomly and unpredictably to maximize their learning (15 mins).

   Remember, you are talking, the students are just listening.

Practice 1

4. Show the students pictures of people from the previous lesson. Combine vocabulary for people and animals in a sentence, such as "The old man bought a monkey." Put the picture of the monkey on top of the picture of the old man as you say this.

5. Encourage the students to try pairing the correct pictures as you give more animal and people combinations (10 min)

Practice 2

6. Place pictures of animals and insects around the room and have the students go to the correct one when you say, "Where is the giraffe?" etc. (10 min).

REPEAT THE NEW VOCABULARY FOR ANIMALS AND INSECTS IN SENTENCES AND THIS TIME HAVE THE STUDENTS RECORD IT ON THEIR PHONES (5 MIN).

Give Homework

Review

Give the students the Weekly Review Template and a copy of the pictures used in the lesson. Tell them to listen to their recordings and practice pointing to the correct pictures during the week. They should transcribe the recordings and try repeating what they hear. Remind them to bring the transcriptions to class for the next lesson for you to check for accuracy.

Community Activity

Give the students the Community Activity Template. Encourage them to observe a common activity in the community during the week.

Actions

You will need
- Pictures of animals and people performing actions
- Weekly Review Template
- Community Activity Template
- Smartphone

Review

Recap last week's lesson and check students' homework activities (10 min).

Vocabulary: stand up, sit down, walk, run, lie down, go, jump, stop, dig, touch, lift, hit, kick, squeeze, pinch, drop, throw, etc.

1. Perform basic actions as you give commands, such as "Stand up" or "Sit down" etc.

2. Have the students join in and perform the actions. Repeat until they have learned ten to twenty new words (15 min).

   Remember to always model the action to the students first, either by doing it yourself or having someone else do it.

Practice 1

3. Play a game using the actions above. Split the students into 2 teams and have each team stand in line. Call out an action, i.e. "Jump." The students at the front of each line must jump from one end of the room to the other, at the end you can say, "You can jump". The first one to perform the action gets their team a point. Continue with more actions for the remaining students.

Practice 2

4. Show the students pictures of people and animals from the previous lesson performing actions.

5. Point to each picture as you state what is happening, "The man is walking" or "He is running."

6. Encourage the students to try pointing to the correct picture as you speak. Repeat until they can recognize the pictures interchangeably (15 mins).

This activity should help the students understand what sentences sound like when they are told what is happening rather than being commanded to do something.

 REPEAT THE NEW VOCABULARY FOR ACTIONS IN SENTENCES AND THIS TIME HAVE THE STUDENTS RECORD IT ON THEIR PHONES (5 MIN).

Give Homework

Review

Give the students the Weekly Review Template and a copy of the pictures used in the lesson. Tell them to listen to their recordings and practice pointing to the correct pictures during the week. They should transcribe the recordings and try repeating what they hear. Remind them to bring the transcriptions to class for the next lesson for you to check for accuracy.

Community Activity

Give the students the Community Activity Template. Encourage them to observe a common activity in the community during the week.

Household Objects

You will need
- Common household objects (or pictures of them)
- Weekly Review Template
- Community Activity Template
- Smartphone

Review

Recap last week's lesson and check students' homework activities (10 min).

Vocabulary: table, chair, fan, TV, mat, basket, kettle, heater, umbrella, computer, bed, lamp, etc.

1. Show the students pictures of common household objects. Point as you say, "Point to the chair" or "Point to the table."

2. The students should imitate you and point to the correct object. Repeat until they can recognize ten to twenty objects interchangeably (15 min).

Practice 1

3. Command the students to touch certain household objects, such as "Touch the basket" or "Touch the knife." Go through as many combinations at random as they can handle (15 min).

Practice 2

4. Place household objects around the classroom and have the students walk around the room and point to the correct one when you say, "Where is the umbrella?" etc. (10 min).

 REPEAT THE NEW VOCABULARY FOR HOUSEHOLD OBJECTS IN SENTENCES AND THIS TIME HAVE THE STUDENTS RECORD IT ON THEIR PHONES (5 MIN).

Give Homework

Review

Give the students the Weekly Review Template and a copy of the pictures used in the lesson. Tell them to listen to their recordings and practice pointing to the correct pictures during the week. They should transcribe the recordings and try repeating what they hear. Remind them to bring the transcriptions to class for the next lesson for you to check for accuracy.

Community Activity

Give the students the Community Activity Template. Encourage them to observe a common activity in the community during the week.

Rooms in a House

You will need
- House Floor Plan
- Pictures of rooms in a house
- Weekly Review Template
- Community Activity Template
- Smartphone

Review

Recap last week's lesson and check students' homework activities (10 min).

Vocabulary: master bedroom, guest bedroom, kitchen, living room, dining room, study, ensuite, walk in robe, garage, patio, hallway, toilet, media room, laundry, foyer, stairs, etc.

1. Show the students pictures of rooms in a house and a floor plan for a house.

2. Point as you say, "Point to the master bedroom" or "Point to the kitchen." Encourage the students to try to point to the correct picture. Repeat until they can recognize ten to twenty pictures interchangeably (10 min).

Practice 1

3. Using the space you are in as a model, begin teaching the common rooms and areas in the building. Beginning with two areas, give commands such as, "Walk to the kitchen" or "Walk to the foyer." Repeat for the remaining rooms in the building until they have learned ten to twenty new words (10 min).

Practice 2

4. Have the students draw a floor plan of their own house.

5. Using vocabulary from the board, encourage the students label each room on their floor plan.

6. Have the students point to the correct room of their floor plan when told, i.e. "Point to the master bathroom" or "Point to the master bedroom" (10 min).

Vocabulary: wall, window, door, floor, roof, ceiling, stairs, rafter, roof beam, eaves, posts, poles, etc.

7. Using the space you are in as a model, have the students respond to simple commands that include words for parts of a building, such as "Point to the pole" or "Point to the ceiling." Repeat for more parts of a building until they have learned ten to twenty new words (5 min).

REPEAT THE NEW VOCABULARY FOR ROOMS IN A HOUSE AND THIS TIME HAVE THE STUDENTS RECORD IT ON THEIR PHONES (5 MIN).

Give Homework

Review

Give the students the Weekly Review Template and a copy of the pictures used in the lesson. Tell them to listen to their recordings and practice pointing to the correct pictures during the week. They should transcribe the recordings and try repeating what they hear. Remind them to bring the transcriptions to class for the next lesson for you to check for accuracy.

Community Activity

Give the students the Community Activity Template. Encourage them to observe a common activity in the community during the week.

Placement Words

You will need
- Pictures of rooms in a house
- Household objects
- Weekly Review Template
- Community Activity Template
- Smartphone

Review

Recap last week's lesson and check students' homework activities (10 min).

Vocabulary: behind, between, in, in front of, next to, on, over, under, below, above, opposite, etc.

1. Using familiar household objects, have the students respond to simple commands that include placement words, such as "Put the spoon in the basket" or "Put the firewood behind the chair." Repeat until they can follow the commands with ease (15 min).

Vocabulary: master bedroom, guest bedroom, kitchen, living room, dining room, study, bathroom, walk in robe, garage, patio, hallway, toilet, media room, laundry, foyer, stairs, etc.

2. Show the students pictures of rooms in a house from the previous lesson. Have them respond to simple to commands that combine placement words with words for rooms in a house, such as "Put the basket next to the bedroom" or "Put the umbrella in front of the kitchen." Repeat until the students can follow the commands with ease (15 min).

Practice

3. Play a game using placement words. Give an object to a student and have them hide it while you leave the room. When you come back, ask yes/no questions to locate it ("Is it near the desk? Is it in the front half of the classroom? Is it under the chair?" etc.). If you have enough English speakers assisting you, try having students play in pairs with them.

> REPEAT THE NEW VOCABULARY FOR PLACEMENTS WORDS IN SENTENCES AND THIS TIME HAVE THE STUDENTS RECORD IT ON THEIR PHONES (5 MIN).

Give Homework

Review

Give the students the Weekly Review Template and a copy of the pictures used in the lesson. Tell them to listen to their recordings and practice pointing to the correct pictures during the week. They should transcribe the recordings and try repeating what they hear. Remind them to bring the transcriptions to class for the next lesson for you to check for accuracy.

Community Activity

Give the students the Community Activity Template. Encourage them to observe a common activity in the community during the week.

The Outdoors

You will need
- Outdoor objects (or pictures of them)
- Pictures of people carrying objects
- Weekly Review Template
- Community Activity Template
- Smartphone

Review

Recap last week's lesson and check students' homework activities (10 min).

Vocabulary: tree, plant, flower, grass, bark, dirt, fence, leaf, branch, pot, shovel, yard, etc.

1. Take the students outside to teach terms for outdoors. Walk to two objects such as flowers and trees and give a command as you do so, such as "Walk to the flower" or "Walk to the tree."

2. Have the students join in and walk to the correct object as you give the command. Repeat until they have learned ten to twenty new words (10 min).

   Instead of always modeling the action yourself, you can also have another English speaker model as you give the command.

Vocabulary: give, pick up, hold, carry, axe, rope etc.

3. Give simple commands to an English speaker that combine terms for carrying and holding with outdoor objects, such as "Give the flower to the woman" or "Pick up the branch."

4. The students should imitate the actions of the English speaker as you give the command. Repeat until they can follow ten to twenty commands interchangeably (10 min).

Vocabulary: sweep, cut, chop, dig, tie, untie, etc.

5. Perform actions related to working with outdoor objects as you give a command, such as "Untie the rope" or "Chop with the axe" or "Dig with the shovel."

6. The students should imitate your actions as you give the command. Start with two actions and gradually add more until they have learned ten to twenty new words (10 min).

Practice

7. Back in the classroom, show the students pictures of people carrying and holding objects.

8. Point as you say, "He is giving the flower to her" or "The woman is giving the pot to the man." Encourage the students to try to point to the correct picture. Repeat until they can recognize the pictures interchangeably (10 mins).

> REPEAT THE NEW VOCABULARY FOR OUTDOOR OBJECTS IN SENTENCES AND THIS TIME HAVE STUDENTS RECORD IT ON THEIR PHONES (5 MIN).

Give Homework

Review

Give the students the Weekly Review Template and a copy of the pictures used in the lesson. Tell them to listen to their recordings and practice pointing to the correct pictures during the week. They should transcribe the recordings and try repeating what they hear. Remind them to bring the transcriptions to class for the next lesson for you to check for accuracy.

Community Activity

Give the students the Community Activity Template. Encourage them to observe a common activity in the community during the week.

LEVEL 1 - BEGINNER Lesson 9

Fruit and Vegetables

You will need
- Plastic fruit and vegetables (or pictures of them)
- Weekly Review Template
- Community Activity Template
- Smartphone

Review

Recap last week's lesson and check students' homework activities (10 min).

Vocabulary: apple, grape, mandarin, celery, carrot, potato, corn, etc.

1. Show the students pictures of fruit and vegetables. Point as you say, "Point to the potato" or "Point to the grape."

2. Encourage the students to try to point to the correct picture. Repeat until the students can recognize up to ten to twenty items interchangeably (15 mins).

Practice 1

3. Combine vocabulary for fruit, vegetables and actions in a sentence, such as "Throw the grape" as you throw the grape.

4. Encourage the students to try performing the actions as you give more fruit, vegetable and action combinations (10 min).

Practice 2

5. Make a fruit salad as a class. Have the students each get fruit for the salad, such as "Get the grapes" then "Put the grapes in the bowl" etc. (10 min).

 REPEAT THE NEW VOCABULARY FOR FRUIT AND VEGETABLES IN SENTENCES AND THIS TIME HAVE THE STUDENTS RECORD IT ON THEIR PHONES (5 MIN).

Give Homework

Review

Give the students the Weekly Review Template and a copy of the pictures used in the lesson. Tell them to listen to their recordings and practice pointing to the correct pictures during the week. They should transcribe the recordings and try repeating what they hear. Remind them to bring the transcriptions to class for the next lesson for you to check for accuracy.

Community Activity

Give the students the Community Activity Template. Encourage them to observe a common activity in the community during the week.

Possession and Ownership

You will need
- Pictures of people
- Common foods (or pictures of them)
- Weekly Review Template
- Community Activity Template
- Smartphone

Review

Recap last week's lesson and check students' homework activities (10 min).

Vocabulary: my, your, our, his, her, its, their, etc.

1. Give each student several food items.

2. Introduce terms for possession and ownership (possessive adjectives). Command an English speaker to perform actions that include possession and ownership, such as "Point to my orange" or "Point to your potato" in which case they would point to the correct item, while responding with a simple sentence, such as "That is your orange."

3. The students should imitate the actions of the English speaker and point to the correct object as you give the command. Repeat until the students recognize the possessive adjectives interchangeably (15 min).

Practice 1

4. The students can try telling you to do the actions above to practice giving commands themselves (5 min).

Practice 2

5. Using vocabulary for carrying and holding from a previous lesson, have an English speaker respond to simple commands that combine terms for carrying and holding with possession and ownership, such as "Give me your potato" or "Pick up his apple."

6. The students should imitate the actions of the English speaker as you give the command. Repeat until they have performed ten to twenty commands (15 min).

REPEAT THE NEW VOCABULARY FOR EATING, POSSESSION AND OWNERSHIP AND THIS TIME HAVE THE STUDENTS RECORD IT ON THEIR PHONES (5 MIN).

Give Homework

Review

Give the students the Weekly Review Template and a copy of the pictures used in the lesson. Tell them to listen to their recordings and practice pointing to the correct pictures during the week. They should transcribe the recordings and try repeating what they hear. Remind them to bring the transcriptions to class for the next lesson for you to check for accuracy.

Community Activity

Give the students the Community Activity Template. Encourage them to observe a common activity in the community during the week.

Singular, Plural and Numbers

You will need
- 55 identical items (such as stones or Lego)
- Pictures of parts of houses
- Weekly Review Template
- Community Activity Template
- Smartphone

Note: For the past 10 lessons the students have been focusing on listening and responding with actions. They can begin to respond with speaking now, imitating the things you say and practice giving appropriate responses.

Review

Recap last week's lesson and check students' homework activities (10 min).

Vocabulary: is, are

1. Using common objects, teach differences in singular and plural. Pose simple questions that include terms for singular and plural, such as "Where is the stone?" or "Where are the sticks?" as you point to the correct object/s.

2. The students should imitate you and give an appropriate response, such as "This is the stone" as they point. Repeat until they can respond to ten to twenty new questions (15 min).

Vocabulary: Numbers 1-10

3. Show the students objects sorted into groups to teach the numbers one to ten (for example, get 55 stones and sort them into groups of one to ten).

4. Point as you say, "Point to three stones" or "Point to five stones."

5. The students should imitate you and give an appropriate response, such as "three stones" as they point. Repeat until the students recognize the numbers 1-10 interchangeably (15 mins).

Practice

6. Using the vocabulary learnt so far, pair students and have them command each other to point to certain groups of objects such as "Point to 10 stones, or point to 1 stone" etc. (5 min).

> REPEAT THE NEW VOCABULARY FOR SINGULAR, PLURAL AND NUMBERS AND THIS TIME HAVE STUDENTS RECORD IT ON THEIR PHONES (5 MIN).

Give Homework

Review

Give the students the Weekly Review Template and a copy of the pictures used in the lesson. Tell them to listen to their recordings and practice pointing to the correct pictures during the week. They should transcribe the recordings and try repeating what they hear. Remind them to bring the transcriptions to class for the next lesson for you to check for accuracy.

Community Activity

Give the students the Community Activity Template. Encourage them to observe a common activity in the community during the week.

Clothing

You will need
- Items of clothing (or pictures of them)
- Pictures of people
- Weekly Review Template
- Community Activity Template
- Smartphone

Review

Recap last week's lesson and check students' homework activities (10 min).

Vocabulary: top, shorts, jeans, jacket, dress, skirt, socks, shoes, pajamas, etc.

1. Show the students pictures of clothing. Starting with two pictures, point as you say, "Point to the dress" or "Point to the shoes."

2. Encourage the students to join in and point to the correct picture as you give the command. Repeat until they have learned ten to twenty new words (10 min).

Practice 1

3. Using the pictures of clothing, have the students respond to simple to commands that combine placement words with words for clothing, such as "Put the socks next to the skirt" or "Put the jacket in front of the shorts." Repeat until the students can follow the commands with ease (10 min).

Practice 2

4. Using pictures of people from a previous lesson, give simple statements that combine terms for kinship with terms for clothes, such as "The father is wearing jeans" or "The grandmother is wearing pajamas" in which case you would point to the correct item of clothing.

5. Have the students join in and point to the correct item of clothing. Go through as many combinations at random as they can handle (10 mins).

Practice 3

6. Using vocabulary learnt so far, pair students and have them command each other to point to certain items of clothing (5 min).

REPEAT THE NEW VOCABULARY FOR CLOTHES IN SENTENCES AND THIS TIME HAVE STUDENTS RECORD IT ON THEIR PHONES (5 MIN).

Give Homework

Review

Give the students the Weekly Review Template and a copy of the pictures used in the lesson. Tell them to listen to their recordings and practice pointing to the correct pictures during the week. They should transcribe the recordings and try repeating what they hear. Remind them to bring the transcriptions to class for the next lesson for you to check for accuracy.

Community Activity

Give the students the Community Activity Template. Encourage them to observe a common activity in the community during the week.

Eating and Cooking

You will need
- Common cooking utensils
- Local foods (or pictures of them)
- Weekly Review Template
- Community Activity Template
- Smartphone

Review

Recap last week's lesson and check students' homework activities (10 min).

Vocabulary: feed, eat, etc.

1. Show the students common food items. Command an English speaker to perform actions that include terms for familiar foods, such as "Eat the lamington" or "Feed me the vegemite."

2. The students should imitate the English speaker and role play feeding and eating. Repeat until the students recognize ten to twenty commands interchangeably (10 min).

Vocabulary: spoon, spatula, saucepan, bowl, knife, chopping board, whisk, measuring cup, tray, etc.

3. Show the students common cooking utensils. Point as you say, "Point to the spoon" or "Point to the whisk."

4. The students should imitate you and point to the correct object. Repeat until they can recognize ten to twenty objects interchangeably (10 min).

Vocabulary: mix, cut, chop, stir, flip, cook, whisk, sift, measure, etc.

5. Expand on the activity above by showing how the utensils are used. Give commands as you perform actions related to the utensil, such as "Mix with the spoon" or "Flip with the spatula."

6. The students should imitate you and perform the action. Repeat until they can recognize ten to twenty commands interchangeably (10 min).

Practice

7. The students can try telling you to do the actions above to practice giving commands themselves (5 min).

REPEAT THE NEW VOCABULARY FOR EATING AND COOKING AND THIS TIME HAVE THE STUDENTS RECORD IT ON THEIR PHONES (5 MIN).

Give Homework

Review

Give the students the Weekly Review Template and a copy of the pictures used in the lesson. Tell them to listen to their recordings and practice pointing to the correct pictures during the week. They should transcribe the recordings and try repeating what they hear. Remind them to bring the transcriptions to class for the next lesson for you to check for accuracy.

Community Activity

Give the students the Community Activity Template. Encourage them to observe a common activity in the community during the week.

Body Parts

You will need
- Pictures of human and animal bodies
- Weekly Review Template
- Community Activity Template
- Smartphone

Review

Recap last week's lesson and check students' homework activities (10 min).

Vocabulary: head, eyes, ears, nose, mouth, neck, shoulder, arms, stomach, legs, feet, etc.

1. Show the students a picture of a person's body. Starting with two body parts, point as you say, "Point to the man's finger" or "Point to the child's head."

2. Encourage the students to join in and point to the correct body parts as you give the command. Repeat until the students have learned ten to twenty new words (10 min).

   Remember, try not to get into the specifics. Stick to the most common terms.

Vocabulary: wings, paws, scales, snout, tail, beak, fins, whiskers, etc.

3. Introduce body parts of animals that are different from people, such as a chicken, dog, snake or fish. Point to the correct body part as you say, "Point to the dog's paw" or "Point to the fish's fins."

4. Encourage the students to join in and point to the correct body part as you give the command. Repeat until they have learnt ten to twenty new words (10 mins).

Practice 1

5. Using pictures of people and animals, give simple commands that combine body parts for people and animals with personal pronouns, such as "Point to his shoulder" or "Point to her leg" or "Point to its tail" (10 mins).

Practice 2

6. Using the vocabulary learned so far, pair the students and have them command each other to point to certain animal and human body parts (5 min).

 REPEAT THE NEW VOCABULARY FOR BODY PARTS IN SENTENCES AND THIS TIME HAVE THE STUDENTS RECORD IT ON THEIR PHONES (5 MIN).

Give Homework

Review

Give the students the Weekly Review Template and a copy of the pictures used in the lesson. Tell them to listen to their recordings and practice pointing to the correct pictures during the week. They should transcribe the recordings and try repeating what they hear. Remind them to bring the transcriptions to class for the next lesson for you to check for accuracy.

Community Activity

Give the students the Community Activity Template. Encourage them to observe a common activity in the community during the week.

Body Positions

You will need
- Pictures of people performing actions
- Weekly Review Template
- Community Activity Template
- Smartphone

Review

Recap last week's lesson and check students' homework activities (10 min).

Vocabulary: kneel, squat, crawl, bend over, lean, lie down, etc.

1. Perform two basic actions related to body positions as you give the command, such as "Kneel" and "Crawl."

2. Encourage the students to join in and perform the action as you give the command. Repeat until they have learned ten to twenty new words (15 mins).

Practice 1

3. The students can try telling you to perform the actions above to practice giving commands themselves (5 min).

Practice 2

4. Using pictures of people performing actions, expand the previous exercise by giving simple commands such as "Point to the man who is kneeling" or "Point to the woman who is crawling."

5. Encourage the students to point to the correct picture as you give the command. Go through as many combinations at random as the students can handle (15 mins).

 REPEAT THE NEW VOCABULARY FOR BODY POSITIONS IN SENTENCES AND THIS TIME HAVE THE STUDENTS RECORD IT ON THEIR PHONES (5 MIN).

Give Homework

Review

Give the students the Weekly Review Template and a copy of the pictures used in the lesson. Tell them to listen to their recordings and practice pointing to the correct pictures during the week. They should transcribe the recordings and try repeating what they hear. Remind them to bring the transcriptions to class for the next lesson for you to check for accuracy.

Community Activity

Give the students the Community Activity Template. Encourage them to observe a common activity in the community during the week.

Family

You will need
- Family Photos
- Family Tree Template
- Weekly Review Template
- Community Activity Template
- Smartphone

Review

Recap last week's lesson and check students' homework activities (10 min).

Vocabulary: father, mother, grandfather, grandmother, wife, son, daughter, uncle, aunt, niece, nephew, father-in-law, mother-in-law, etc.

1. Show the students a photo of your family. Starting with two family members, point as you say, "Point to my mother" or "Point to my father."

2. Encourage the students to join in and point to the correct person as you give the command. Repeat until they have learned ten to twenty new words (10 min).

Practice 1

3. If you have English speakers assisting you, pair the students with them. Have them show each other a photo of their family. Encourage them to point to each family member and introduce them, such as "This is my mother" or "This is my niece" (10 min).

Practice 2

4. Have the students draw their family tree and label with the correct kinship terms.

5. Using the family tree, encourage the students to point to the correct relatives as you give the command such as, "Point to your grandfather on your mother's side" or "Point to your aunt on your father's side" or "Point to your cousins" (20 min).

REPEAT THE NEW VOCABULARY FOR KINSHIP IN SENTENCES AND THIS TIME HAVE THE STUDENTS RECORD IT ON THEIR PHONES (5 MIN).

Give Homework

Review

Give the students the Weekly Review Template and a copy of the pictures used in the lesson. Tell them to listen to their recordings and practice pointing to the correct pictures during the week. They should transcribe the recordings and try repeating what they hear. Remind them to bring the transcriptions to class for the next lesson for you to check for accuracy.

Community Activity

Give the students the Community Activity Template. Encourage them to observe a common activity in the community during the week.

Opposites

You will need
- Objects that represent opposites
- Weekly Review Template
- Community Activity Template
- Smartphone

Review

Recap last week's lesson and check students' homework activities (10 min).

Vocabulary: large/small, heavy/light, long/short, hot/cold, rough/smooth, tall/short, thick/thin, round/flat, etc.

1. Show the students objects that represent a variety of adjective pair opposites, such as a stone and a feather for heavy/light, a long and short bamboo skewer for long/short, a square of paper and sandpaper for rough/smooth or a round and flat stone for round/flat, etc.

2. Beginning with two objects, point as you say, "Point to the thing that is thin" or "Point to the thing that is hot."

3. The students should imitate you and give an appropriate response, such as "This is hot" as they point. Repeat until they have learnt ten to twenty new words for opposites (15 mins).

Practice 1

4. Using objects that represent opposites, have the students respond to simple commands that combine placement words with opposites, such as "Put the large thing next to the long thing" or "Put the heavy thing on top of the flat thing." Repeat until they can follow the commands with ease (15 min).

Practice 2

5. Using the vocabulary learned so far, pair the students and have them command each other to point to certain objects (5 min).

REPEAT THE NEW VOCABULARY FOR OPPOSITES AND THIS TIME HAVE THE STUDENTS RECORD IT ON THEIR PHONES (5 MIN).

Give Homework

Review

Give the students the Weekly Review Template and a copy of the pictures used in the lesson. Tell them to listen to their recordings and practice pointing to the correct pictures during the week. They should transcribe the recordings and try repeating what they hear. Remind them to bring the transcriptions to class for the next lesson for you to check for accuracy.

Community Activity

Give the students the Community Activity Template. Encourage them to observe a common activity in the community during the week.

Colors

You will need
- Objects that represent colors
- Weekly Review Template
- Community Activity Template
- Smartphone

Review

Recap last week's lesson and check students' homework activities (10 min).

Vocabulary: red, blue, green, yellow, pink, purple, orange, black, brown, white, etc.

1. Show the students objects that represent a variety of colors, such as cups, Lego or crayons. Starting with two objects, point as you say, "Point to the blue cup" or "Point to the red cup."

2. The students should imitate you and give an appropriate response, such as "This is the red cup" as they point. Repeat until they can recognize all the common colors (15 min).

Practice 1

3. Using colored objects (ideally the same object but in different colors), have the students respond to simple to commands that combine placement words with colors, such as "Put the red cup next to the blue cup" or "Put the yellow cup on top of the green cup." Repeat until the students can follow the commands with ease (10 min).

Practice 2

4. Using the vocabulary learned so far, pair the students and have them command each other to point to certain objects (5 min).

 REPEAT THE NEW VOCABULARY FOR COLORS AND THIS TIME HAVE THE STUDENTS RECORD IT ON THEIR PHONES (5 MIN).

Give Homework

Review

Give the students the Weekly Review Template and a copy of the pictures used in the lesson. Tell them to listen to their recordings and practice pointing to the correct pictures during the week. They should transcribe the recordings and try repeating what they hear. Remind them to bring the transcriptions to class for the next lesson for you to check for accuracy.

Community Activity

Give the students the Community Activity Template. Encourage them to observe a common activity in the community during the week.

Give and Take

You will need
- Assortment of familiar objects
- Pouring containers, cups and liquids
- Pictures of landforms and bodies of water
- Whiteboard & marker

Review

Recap last week's lesson and check students' homework activities (10 min).

Vocabulary: throw, show, take, bring, give, etc.

1. Command an English speaker to perform actions related to familiar objects, such as "Throw the rock to me" or "Give the basket to him" or "Take the basket from him." The English speaker should repeat the command as they perform the action.

2. Have the students join in and repeat the command as they perform the action.

3. Repeat until they have learned ten to twenty new words (15 min).

Practice

4. The students can try telling you to do the actions above to practice giving commands themselves (10 min).

Vocabulary: drink, sip, gulp, dump, spill, splash, sprinkle, pour, tip, etc.

5. Using a pouring container and a cup, introduce terms for actions to do with various liquids. Give simple commands related to liquids, such as "Pour some coffee" or "Dump out the water."

6. Have the students join in and repeat the command as they perform the action. Repeat until they have learned ten to twenty new words (15 mins).

Vocabulary: ocean, river, lake, pond, island, hill, mountain, valley, plain, etc.

7. Show the students pictures of landforms and bodies of water. Point as you say, "Point to the ocean" or "Point to the island."

8. The students should imitate you and give an appropriate response, such as "This is the island" as they point. Repeat until they have leaned 10-20 new words (15 min).

> REPEAT THE NEW VOCABULARY FOR GIVE AND TAKE, LIQUIDS, LANDFORMS AND BODIES OF WATER AND THIS TIME HAVE THE STUDENTS RECORD IT ON THEIR PHONES (5 MIN).

Give Homework

Review

Give the students the Weekly Review Template and a copy of the pictures used in the lesson. Tell them to listen to their recordings and practice pointing to the correct pictures during the week. They should transcribe the recordings and try repeating what they hear. Remind them to bring the transcriptions to class for the next lesson for you to check for accuracy.

Community Activity

Give the students the Community Activity Template. Encourage them to observe a common activity in the community during the week.

Time

You will need
- Calendars & clocks for each student
- Weekly Review Template
- Community Activity Template
- Smartphone

Review

Recap last week's lesson and check students' homework activities (10 min).

Vocabulary: today, tomorrow, yesterday, day before, day after, etc.

1. Show the students a calendar. Draw an 'X' on the current date. Point as you say, "Point to today" or "Point to yesterday."

2. Give the students calendars and encourage them to imitate you and give an appropriate response, such as "This is today" as they point to the correct date. Repeat until they have learned ten to twenty new words (10 min).

Vocabulary: Sunday, Monday, Tuesday, Wednesday, Thursday, Friday, Saturday

3. Expand the exercise above by teaching days of the week. Starting with two terms, point to the correct date on the calendar as you say, "Today is Wednesday" or "Yesterday was Tuesday."

4. The students should imitate you and repeat the sentence as they point to the correct date. Repeat until they have learnt all the days of the week (10 min).

Vocabulary: O'clock

5. Combine numbers and time by teaching clock times. Using an example clock, say "It is 2 o'clock" and mark the time on the clock.

6. Encourage the students to join in and mark the time on the clock as they repeat the sentence "It is 2 o'clock." Repeat until they have practiced all twelve hours (10 min).

Vocabulary: January, February, March, April, May, June, July, August, September, October, November, December

7. Using the calendar again, open to the correct month as you say, "Point to January" or "Point to February."

8. The students should imitate you and give an appropriate response, such as "This is January" as they open to the correct months on their calendars. Repeat until they recognize all twelve months interchangeably (5 mins).

> REPEAT THE NEW VOCABULARY FOR TIME AND HAVE THE STUDENTS RECORD IT ON THEIR PHONES (5 MIN).

Give Homework

Review

Give the students the Weekly Review Template and a copy of the pictures used in the lesson. Tell them to listen to their recordings and practice pointing to the correct pictures during the week. They should transcribe the recordings and try repeating what they hear. Remind them to bring the transcriptions to class for the next lesson for you to check for accuracy.

Community Activity

Give the students the Community Activity Template. Encourage them to observe a common activity in the community during the week.

Seasons and Weather

You will need
- Pictures of the sky, weather & seasons
- Calendars for students
- Weekly Review Template
- Community Activity Template
- Smartphone

Review

Recap last week's lesson and check students' homework activities (10 min).

Vocabulary: sun, sky, moon, stars, clouds, rain, mist, fog, wind, etc.

1. Show the students pictures related to the sky and weather. Starting with two pictures, point as you say, "Point to the sun" or "Point to the clouds."

2. The students should imitate you and give an appropriate response, such as "This is the sun" as they point to the correct picture. Repeat until they have learned ten to twenty new words (10 min).

Vocabulary: summer, winter, spring, autumn/fall

3. Show the students pictures that represent the seasons. Starting with two pictures, point as you say, "Point to summer" or "Point to winter."

4. The students should imitate you and give an appropriate response, such as "This is summer" as they point. Repeat until they recognize all four seasons interchangeably (10 mins).

Practice 1

5. Look at the weekly weather forecast. Using pictures of symbols that represent different kinds of weather, point as you say "Point to the sunny day, cloudy rainy, etc."

6. The students should imitate you and give an appropriate response, such as "This is a cloudy day" as they point (10 min).

Practice 2

7. Using vocabulary learned so far, pair the students and have them command each other to point to certain pictures of weather and seasons (10 min).

 REPEAT THE NEW VOCABULARY FOR SEASONS AND WEATHER AND THIS TIME HAVE THE STUDENTS RECORD IT ON THEIR PHONES (5 MIN).

Give Homework

Review

Give the students the Weekly Review Template and a copy of the pictures used in the lesson. Tell them to listen to their recordings and practice pointing to the correct pictures during the week. They should transcribe the recordings and try repeating what they hear. Remind them to bring the transcriptions to class for the next lesson for you to check for accuracy.

Community Activity

Give the students the Community Activity Template. Encourage them to observe a common activity in the community during the week.

Emotions

You will need
- Pictures of emotions
- Assortment of familiar objects
- Weekly Review Template
- Community Activity Template
- Smartphone

Review

Recap last week's lesson and check students' homework activities (10 min).

Vocabulary: sad, happy, angry, scared, surprised, excited, crying, disgusted, curious, etc.

1. Show the students pictures related to people's emotions. Starting with two pictures, point as you say, "Point to the angry man" or "Point to the happy person."

2. The students should imitate you and give an appropriate response as they point to the correct picture, such as "This is the angry man." Repeat until they have learned ten to twenty new words (15 min).

Practice 1

3. Give simple commands that combine familiar objects with emotional states of individuals, such as "Give the rock to the sad man."

4. The students would then place the rock on top of the picture of the sad man as they give an appropriate response, such as "Here is the rock." Go through as many combinations at random as the students can handle (15 mins).

Practice 2

5. Using the vocabulary learned so far, pair the students and have them command each other to point to certain pictures of emotions (5 min).

REPEAT THE NEW VOCABULARY FOR EMOTIONS AND THIS TIME HAVE THE STUDENTS RECORD IT ON THEIR PHONES (5 MIN).

Give Homework

Review

Give the students the Weekly Review Template and a copy of the pictures used in the lesson. Tell them to listen to their recordings and practice pointing to the correct pictures during the week. They should transcribe the recordings and try repeating what they hear. Remind them to bring the transcriptions to class for the next lesson for you to check for accuracy.

Community Activity

Give the students the Community Activity Template. Encourage them to observe a common activity in the community during the week.

Animal & Insect Behavior

You will need
- Pictures of animals and insects
- Weekly Review Template
- Community Activity Template
- Smartphone

Review

Recap last week's lesson and check students' homework activities (10 min).

Vocabulary: centipede, beetle, wasp, fly, caterpillar, butterfly, ant, cockroach, mosquito, etc.

1. Show the students pictures of common insects. Starting with two pictures, point as you say, "Point to the caterpillar" or "Point to the fly."

2. The students should imitate you and give an appropriate response as they point to the correct picture, such as "This is the fly." Repeat until they have learned ten to twenty new words (15 min).

Vocabulary: sting, bite, strike, bite, hiss, bark, growl, cluck, scratch, crow, swim, fly, etc.

3. Using pictures of insects and animals, introduce terms related to animal and insect behaviors, such as "Centipedes sting" or "Dogs bite."

4. The students should imitate you and repeat the sentence as they point to the correct picture. Repeat until they have learnt ten to twenty new words (15 min).

Practice

5. Using the vocabulary learned so far, pair the students and have them command each other to point to certain pictures of animals and insects (5 min).

 REPEAT THE NEW VOCABULARY FOR ANIMALS AND INSECTS AND THIS TIME HAVE THE STUDENTS RECORD IT ON THEIR PHONES (5 MIN).

Give Homework

Review

Give the students the Weekly Review Template and a copy of the pictures used in the lesson. Tell them to listen to their recordings and practice pointing to the correct pictures during the week. They should transcribe the recordings and try repeating what they hear. Remind them to bring the transcriptions to class for the next lesson for you to check for accuracy.

Community Activity

Give the students the Community Activity Template. Encourage them to observe a common activity in the community during the week.

Shopping

You will need
- Items in a grocery store (or pictures of them)
- Map of a grocery store
- Weekly Review Template
- Community Activity Template
- Smartphone

Review

Recap last week's lesson and check students' homework activities (10 min).

Vocabulary: conveyer belt, checkout counter, checkout operator, shopping cart, basket, shopping list, reusable bags, grocery store, etc.

1. Show the students pictures of items they are likely to see in a grocery store.

2. Point as you say, "Point to the checkout operator" or "Point to the basket." Encourage the students to try to point to the correct picture. Repeat until they can recognize ten to twenty items interchangeably (10 min).

Vocabulary: fruit & vegetables, deli, bakery, grocery aisles, home & beauty, freezer and refrigerated section

3. Give the students a map of the different sections in a grocery store.

4. Point as you say, "Point to the fruit and vegetable section" or "Point to the deli." Encourage students to try to point to the correct picture. Repeat until the students can recognize the sections interchangeably (10 min).

Practice 1

5. Expand on the previous activity by placing signs around the room with the various sections in a grocery store.

6. Pick up a grocery item and ask a question, i.e. "This is an apple. Where can you get it?"

7. Have the students move in front of the correct sign, i.e. the fruit and vegetable section (10 min).

Practice 2

8. Pair the students and give them a map and some groceries.

9. Have one student pick up a grocery item and ask a question, i.e. "This is a bread roll. Where can you get it?"

10. Have the other student point to the section on their store map where the item comes from, i.e. the bakery section (5 min).

> REPEAT THE NEW VOCABULARY FOR ITEMS IN A GROCERY STORE AND THIS TIME HAVE THE STUDENTS RECORD IT ON THEIR PHONES (5 MIN).

Give Homework

Review

Give the students the Weekly Review Template and a copy of the pictures used in the lesson. Tell them to listen to their recordings and practice pointing to the correct pictures during the week. They should transcribe the recordings and try repeating what they hear. Remind them to bring the transcriptions to class for the next lesson for you to check for accuracy.

Community Activity

Give the students the Community Activity Template. Encourage them to observe a common activity in the community during the week.

Medical

You will need
- Medical items (or pictures of them)
- Pictures of things related to a medical center
- Weekly Review Template
- Community Activity Template
- Smartphone

Review

Recap last week's lesson and check students' homework activities (10 min).

Vocabulary: medical center, doctor, nurse, receptionist, pharmacy, script, waiting room, etc.

1. Show the students pictures of things related to a medical center.

2. Point as you say, "Point to the doctor" or "Point to the script." Encourage the students to try to point to the correct picture. Repeat until they can recognize ten to twenty items interchangeably (10 min).

Vocabulary: band-aids, wheelchair, crutches, tablets, needle, thermometer, bandage, medicine, mask, stethoscope, first aid kit, etc.

3. Show the students pictures of medical items.

4. Point as you say, "Point to the tablets" or "Point to the needle." Encourage the students to try to point to the correct picture. Repeat until they can recognize ten to twenty items interchangeably (10 min).

Practice 1

5. Expand on the previous activity by placing medical items around the room.

6. Give commands such as, "Walk to the thermometer" or "Walk to the mask." Repeat for the remaining items until the students can recognize the items interchangeably (10 min).

Practice 2

7. The students can try telling you to do the actions above to practice giving commands themselves (5 min).

> REPEAT THE NEW VOCABULARY FOR ITEMS IN A MEDICAL CENTER AND THIS TIME HAVE THE STUDENTS RECORD IT ON THEIR PHONES (5 MIN).

Give Homework

Review

Give the students the Weekly Review Template and a copy of the pictures used in the lesson. Tell them to listen to their recordings and practice pointing to the correct pictures during the week. They should transcribe the recordings and try repeating what they hear. Remind them to bring the transcriptions to class for the next lesson for you to check for accuracy.

Community Activity

Give the students the Community Activity Template. Encourage them to observe a common activity in the community during the week.

School

You will need
- Items in a school/university (or pictures of them)
- Map of a school/university
- Weekly Review Template
- Community Activity Template
- Smartphone

Review

Recap last week's lesson and check students' homework activities (10 min).

Vocabulary: classroom, university, cafeteria, library, medical labs, gym, computer labs, etc.

1. Show the students a map of places they are likely to come across in a school or university.

2. Point as you say, "Point to the library" or "Point to the computer labs." Encourage the students to try to point to the correct place on the map. Repeat until they can recognize ten to twenty items interchangeably (10 min).

Practice 1

3. Expand on the previous activity by placing signs around the room with the various places in a school or university.

4. Give commands such as, "Walk to the library" or "Walk to the computer labs." Repeat for the remaining items until the students can recognize the items interchangeably (10 min).

Vocabulary: notebook, pen, whiteboard, marker, eraser, desk, laptop, water bottle, student, teacher, textbooks, etc.

5. Show the students pictures of school/university items.

6. Point as you say, "Point to the marker" or "Point to the notebook." Encourage the students to try to point to the correct picture. Repeat until they can recognize ten to twenty items interchangeably (10 min).

Practice 2

7. Using the vocabulary learned so far, pair the students and have them command each other to point to certain pictures of school/university items (10 min).

> REPEAT THE NEW VOCABULARY FOR ITEMS IN A SCHOOL/UNIVERSITY AND THIS TIME HAVE THE STUDENTS RECORD IT ON THEIR PHONES (5 MIN).

Give Homework

Review

Give the students the Weekly Review Template and a copy of the pictures used in the lesson. Tell them to listen to their recordings and practice pointing to the correct pictures during the week. They should transcribe the recordings and try repeating what they hear. Remind them to bring the transcriptions to class for the next lesson for you to check for accuracy.

Community Activity

Give the students the Community Activity Template. Encourage them to observe a common activity in the community during the week.

Tools

You will need
- Tools (or pictures of them)
- Weekly Review Template
- Community Activity Template
- Smartphone

Review

Recap last week's lesson and check students' homework activities (10 min).

Vocabulary: hammer, nail, screwdriver, screw, drill, shovel, pliers, saw, nail gun, rake, axe, etc.

1. Show the students tools (or pictures of them).

2. Point as you say, "Point to the screw" or "Point to the axe." Encourage the students to try to point to the correct picture. Repeat until they can recognize ten to twenty items interchangeably (10 min).

Practice 1

3. If possible, take the students outside and place tools around an outdoor area.

4. Give commands such as, "Walk to the shovel" or "Walk to the pliers." Repeat for the remaining items until the students can recognize the items interchangeably (10 min).

Vocabulary: hit, screw, drill, dig, rake, nail, cut, chop, etc.

5. Expand on the previous activity by having the students perform actions related to the tools as you give a command, such as "Dig with the shovel" or "Chop with the axe" or "Drill with the drill."

6. The students should imitate you as you give the command. Start with two actions and gradually add more until they have learned ten to twenty new words (10 min).

Practice 2

7. Back in the classroom, pair students and have them command each other to perform actions related to tools (5 min).

REPEAT THE NEW VOCABULARY FOR TOOLS AND THIS TIME HAVE THE STUDENTS RECORD IT ON THEIR PHONES (5 MIN).

Give Homework

Review

Give the students the Weekly Review Template and a copy of the pictures used in the lesson. Tell them to listen to their recordings and practice pointing to the correct pictures during the week. They should transcribe the recordings and try repeating what they hear. Remind them to bring the transcriptions to class for the next lesson for you to check for accuracy.

Community Activity

Give the students the Community Activity Template. Encourage them to observe a common activity in the community during the week.

Travel

You will need

- Pictures related to travel and transport
- Weekly Review Template
- Community Activity Template
- Smartphone

Review

Recap last week's lesson and check students' homework activities (10 min).

Vocabulary: train, bus, plane, motorbike, car, ferry, ship, taxi, etc.

1. Show the students pictures of common modes of transport.

2. Point as you say, "Point to the taxi" or "Point to the bus." Encourage the students to try to point to the correct picture. Repeat until they can recognize ten to twenty items interchangeably (10 min).

Practice 1

3. Using the vocabulary learned so far, pair the students and have them command each other to point to certain modes of transport (5 min).

Vocabulary: ticket, platform, train station, bus stop, flight attendant, captain, terminal, visa, first class, business class, economy, overhead lockers, baggage claim, arrival and departure screen, etc.

4. Show the students pictures related to transport and travel.

5. Point as you say, "Point to the visa" or "Point to the captain." Encourage the students to try to point to the correct picture. Repeat until they can recognize ten to twenty items interchangeably (10 min).

Practice 2

6. Expand on the previous activity by placing travel pictures around the room.

7. Give commands such as, "Walk to first class" or "Walk to the train station". Repeat for the remaining items until the students can recognize the items interchangeably (10 min).

REPEAT THE NEW VOCABULARY FOR ITEMS IN TRANSPORT/TRAVEL AND THIS TIME HAVE THE STUDENTS RECORD IT ON THEIR PHONES (5 MIN).

Give Homework

Review

Give the students the Weekly Review Template and a copy of the pictures used in the lesson. Tell them to listen to their recordings and practice pointing to the correct pictures during the week. They should transcribe the recordings and try repeating what they hear. Remind them to bring the transcriptions to class for the next lesson for you to check for accuracy.

Community Activity

Give the students the Community Activity Template. Encourage them to observe a common activity in the community during the week.

Sport

You will need
- Pictures of common sports
- Sporting items, such as a soccer ball, bike, etc.
- Weekly Review Template
- Community Activity Template
- Smartphone

Review

Recap last week's lesson and check students' homework activities (10 min).

Vocabulary: basketball, soccer, hockey, ice skating, bike riding, running, hiking, swimming, kayaking, cricket, etc.

1. Show the students pictures of different sports.

2. Point as you say, "Point to cricket" or "Point to swimming." Encourage the students to try to point to the correct picture. Repeat until they can recognize ten to twenty items interchangeably (10 min).

Practice 1

3. Expand on the previous activity by placing sporting pictures around the room.

4. Give commands such as, "Walk to soccer" or "Walk to basketball." Repeat for the remaining items until the students can recognize the items interchangeably (10 min).

Vocabulary: shoot the basketball, kick the soccer ball, ride the bike, run, hike, swim, etc.

5. If possible, take the students outside and have them perform actions related to the sport as you give a command, such as "Run" or "Kick the soccer ball" or "Shoot the basketball." You can either use real objects to help with the actions (i.e. provide a real basketball and hoop) or just else just pretend to do the action.

6. The students should imitate you as you give the command. Start with two actions and gradually add more until they have learned ten to twenty new words (10 min).

Practice 2

Pair students and have them command each other to perform actions related to sports (5 min).

 REPEAT THE NEW VOCABULARY FOR SPORT AND THIS TIME HAVE THE STUDENTS RECORD IT ON THEIR PHONES (5 MIN).

Give Homework

Review

Give the students the Weekly Review Template and a copy of the pictures used in the lesson. Tell them to listen to their recordings and practice pointing to the correct pictures during the week. They should transcribe the recordings and try repeating what they hear. Remind them to bring the transcriptions to class for the next lesson for you to check for accuracy.

Community Activity

Give the students the Community Activity Template. Encourage them to observe a common activity in the community during the week.

Entertainment

You will need
- Assortment of Books (or pictures of them)
- Pictures related to movies and the theatre
- Weekly Review Template
- Community Activity Template
- Smartphone

Review

Recap last week's lesson and check students' homework activities (10 min).

Vocabulary: play, theater, television, stage, actor, cartoon, romance, action, documentary, drama, etc.

1. Show the students pictures related to movies and the theatre.

2. Point as you say, "Point to the actor" or "Point to the documentary." Encourage the students to try to point to the correct picture. Repeat until they can recognize ten to twenty items interchangeably (10 min).

Practice 1

3. Using the vocabulary learned so far, pair the students and have them command each other to point to certain pictures (5 min).

Vocabulary: book, textbook, comics, cookbook, atlas, journal, biography, novel, magazine, newspaper, fiction, non-fiction, poetry, etc.

4. Show the students an assortment of books (or pictures of them).

5. Point as you say, "Point to the magazine" or "Point to the atlas." Encourage the students to try to point to the correct picture. Repeat until they can recognize ten to twenty items interchangeably (10 min).

Practice 2

6. Expand on the previous activity by placing books around the room.

7. Give commands such as, "Walk to the novel" or "Walk to the cookbook." Repeat for the remaining items until the students can recognize the items interchangeably (10 min).

> REPEAT THE NEW VOCABULARY FOR ENTERTAINMENT AND THIS TIME HAVE THE STUDENTS RECORD IT ON THEIR PHONES (5 MIN).

Give Homework

Review

Give the students the Weekly Review Template and a copy of the pictures used in the lesson. Tell them to listen to their recordings and practice pointing to the correct pictures during the week. They should transcribe the recordings and try repeating what they hear. Remind them to bring the transcriptions to class for the next lesson for you to check for accuracy.

Community Activity

Give the students the Community Activity Template. Encourage them to observe a common activity in the community during the week.

LEVEL 2 - BEGINNER

Attending ESL Class

You will need
- Pen
- Notebook
- Weekly Review Template
- Smartphone

Note: In Level 2 the students can look back on the community activities they observed as part of their Homework in Level 1. Any photos they took will be helpful as they carry out the routines themselves in Level 2.

Review

Recap last week's lesson and check students' homework activities (10 min).

Attending ESL Class Routine

1. Pack your smartphone, pen, and notebook.

2. When you arrive, say "Hi" to everyone.

3. Be ready to join in and try speaking.

4. The teacher might ask you to work with a helper or with the other students.

5. The teacher will give you homework for the week. Ask any questions you might have.

6. Take a recording of the teacher using the new words you have learned.

7. There might be time for tea or coffee and a snack. It's a good time to try talking with the other students and helpers.

8. There might be time for a Bible story, you can stay and listen if you like.

9. When you are ready to leave, say "Goodbye."

10. Remember to do your homework! The more you practice, the faster you will learn. Try to spend lots of time with people during the week so you learn the local way of doing things.

11. Find a helper who can speak your language and English. They can help you with your homework.

1. Ask the students "What would you like to learn in English class this term?" (5 min).

2. Go through the routine (10 min).

3. Go through the routine again quickly and this time have the students record it on their phones (5 min).

4. As a class, role play the process of attending ESL class (15 min).

5. Describe an aspect of the setting, such as the classroom, and have the students record the description on their phones, i.e. "The classroom has desks with seats. There is a whiteboard at the front and an air conditioner at the back. There are shelves with pens, paper and whiteboard markers. There are extra seats stacked up at the back, etc."(5 min).

6. Have the students take a photo of the setting to remind them of it when they are reviewing the routine for Homework later.

 STUDENTS TO LISTEN TO RECORDINGS WITH AN ENGLISH SPEAKER. TELL THEM TO STOP THE RECORDINGS IF THERE ARE ANY WORDS THEY DON'T UNDERSTAND FOR THE ENGLISH SPEAKER TO EXPLAIN (10 MIN).

Note: If you have enough English speakers assisting in class, you can pair them with students, and they can listen to the recordings together in class. If not, you can give this to students to do as Homework during the week with their designated language helper.

Give Homework

 Give the students the Weekly Review Template and a copy of the pictures used in the lesson. Tell them to listen to their recordings and practice pointing to the correct pictures during the week. They should transcribe the recordings and try repeating what they hear. Remind them to bring the transcriptions to class for the next lesson for you to check for accuracy.

Note: Students should listen to their recordings twice. The first time they should try to write down what they hear and the second time they should try repeating what they hear, sentence by sentence. See instructions for transcribing recordings on page 10.

*If students are illiterate then do not ask them to transcribe the recordings.

Attending ESL Class

1. Pack your smartphone, pen, and notebook.

2. When you arrive, say hi to everyone.

3. Be ready to join in and try speaking.

4. The teacher might ask you to work with a helper or with the other students.

5. The teacher will give you homework for the week. Ask any questions you might have.

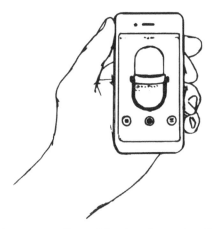

6. Take a recording of the teacher using the new words you have learned.

7 There might be time for tea or coffee and a snack. Try talking with the other students and helpers.

8 There might be time for a Bible story, you can stay and listen if you like.

9 When you are ready to leave, say goodbye.

10 Remember to do your homework! The more you practice, the faster you will learn. Try to spend lots of time with people during the week so you learn the local way of doing things.

11 Find a helper who can speak your language and English. They can help you with your homework.

 ## Give Homework

Listen to the recording again and try repeating what you hear, sentence by sentence. See if you can also point to the correct pictures/perform the correct action as you repeat the recording. Remember to bring this to class with you next week!

Getting Public Transport

You will need
- Travel card or train ticket
- Weekly Review Template
- Smartphone

Review

Recap last week's lesson and check students' homework activities (10 min).

Getting Public Transport Routine

1. Go to the website for the transport of your choice, such as the train. Find the best website for the country you are in. Trip Planner is a good website for Australia.

2. Type in the details of your trip, i.e. your location and destination.

3. Choose the option that suits you best. It will show you the details for your trip.

4. Arrive at the station a few minutes early.

5. Buy your ticket or travel card at the ticket office.

6. Look at the screens above the platform to find the details of your train.

7. Stand on the correct platform.

8. When the train stops, wait for the people to get out.

9. Step into the train and sit down.

10. Get out when you hear your destination called.

1. Ask the students "What public transport do you take?" (5 min).

2. Go through the routine (10 min).

3. Go through the routine again quickly and this time have the students record it on their phones (5 min).

4. As a class or in pairs, role play catching a train (15 min).

5. Describe an aspect of the setting, such as the train, and have the students record the description on their phones, i.e. "The train has two levels. One level is upstairs, and one is downstairs. The seats near the door are for disabled people, old people or women who are pregnant. The train has handles to hold on to when it is moving. The handle stops you from falling."

6. Have the students take a photo of the setting to remind them of it when they are reviewing the routine for Homework later (5 min).

 STUDENTS TO LISTEN TO RECORDINGS WITH AN ENGLISH SPEAKER. TELL THEM TO STOP THE RECORDINGS IF THERE ARE ANY WORDS THEY DON'T UNDERSTAND FOR THE ENGLISH SPEAKER TO EXPLAIN (10 MIN).

Give Homework

 Give the students the Weekly Review Template and a copy of the pictures used in the lesson. Tell them to listen to their recordings and practice pointing to the correct pictures during the week. They should transcribe the recordings and try repeating what they hear. Remind them to bring the transcriptions to class for the next lesson for you to check for accuracy.

Getting Public Transport

1. Go to the website for the transport of your choice, i.e. train.

2. Type in the details of your trip, i.e. your location and destination.

3. Choose the option that suits you best. It will show you the details for your trip.

4. Arrive at the station a few minutes early.

5. Buy your ticket or travel card at the ticket office.

6. Look at the screens above the platform to find out the details of your train.

7 Stand on the correct platform.

8 When the train stops, wait for the people to get out.

9 Step into the train and sit down.

10 Get out when you hear your destination called.

Give Homework

> LISTEN TO YOUR RECORDING OF THE TEACHER GIVING THE STEPS FOR GETTING PUBLIC TRANSPORT AND WRITE DOWN WHAT YOU HEAR.

Listen to the recording again and try repeating what you hear, sentence by sentence. See if you can also point to the correct pictures/perform the correct action as you repeat the recording. Remember to bring this to class with you next week!

....

....

....

....

Washing Dishes

You will need
- Kitchen and items for washing dishes
- Weekly Review Template
- Smartphone

Review

Recap last week's lesson and check students' homework activities (10 min).

Washing Dishes Routine

1. Scrape any food off the dishes.
2. Put on gloves for protection.
3. Fill the sink with hot water.
4. Pour dish washing liquid into the sink.
5. Dip each dish in soapy water and scrub with a sponge.
6. Remember to leave the dirtiest dishes till last.
7. Rinse the dishes in cold water to remove the soap.
8. Drain and refill the sink if the water gets dirty.
9. Put the dishes on a rack to dry.

1. Ask the students "Who washes the dishes at your house?" (5 min).
2. Go through the routine (10 min).
3. Go through the routine again quickly and this time have the students record it on their phones (5 min).
4. Wash dishes as a class in the kitchen (15 min)

5. Describe the process of washing dishes and have the students record the description on their phones, i.e. "The sink is a large rectangle shape. It has a cold and hot water tap. The dish washing liquid is yellow and smells like lemons. The water was very dirty after we washed the dishes. We left the dishes on a metal dish rack to dry, etc" (5 min).

6. Have the students take a photo of the setting to remind them of it when they are reviewing the routine for Homework later (5 min).

 STUDENTS TO LISTEN TO RECORDINGS WITH AN ENGLISH SPEAKER. TELL THEM TO STOP THE RECORDINGS IF THERE ARE ANY WORDS THEY DON'T UNDERSTAND FOR THE ENGLISH SPEAKER TO EXPLAIN (10 MIN).

Give Homework

 Give the students the Weekly Review Template and a copy of the pictures used in the lesson. Tell them to listen to their recordings and practice pointing to the correct pictures during the week. They should transcribe the recordings and try repeating what they hear. Remind them to bring the transcriptions to class for the next lesson for you to check for accuracy.

 **Community Life** ESL

Washing Dishes

1 Scrape any food off the dishes.

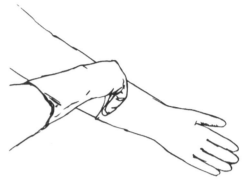

2 Put on gloves for protection.

3 Fill the sink with hot water.

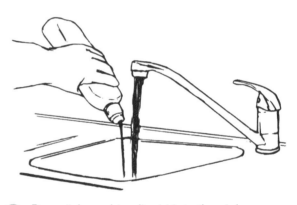

4 Pour dish washing liquid into the sink.

5 Dip each dish in soapy water and scrub with a sponge.

6 Remember to leave the dirtiest dishes till last.

 Rinse the dishes in cold water.

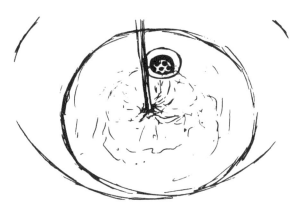

Drain and refill the sink if the water gets dirty.

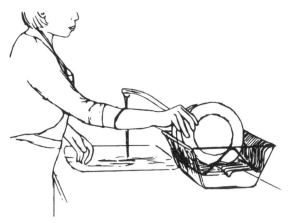

 Put the dishes on a rack to dry.

 ## Give Homework

> LISTEN TO YOUR RECORDING OF THE TEACHER GIVING THE STEPS FOR WASHING DISHES AND WRITE DOWN WHAT YOU HEAR.

Listen to the recording again and try repeating what you hear, sentence by sentence. See if you can also point to the correct pictures/perform the correct action as you repeat the recording. Remember to bring this to class with you next week!

Washing Clothes

You will need
- Access to a washing machine
- Items for washing clothes, such as washing detergent and fabric softener
- Weekly Review Template
- Smartphone

Review

Recap last week's lesson and check students' homework activities (10 min).

Washing Clothes Routine

1. Sort your clothes into piles. It is best to wash clothes of the same color together, especially dark or light clothes.

2. Read the 'care tag' on your clothes, it gives you information about your clothes.

3. Set the right temperature. Hot water is best for dirty clothes, but cold water is best for dark colors, so that the dye doesn't come out.

4. Select the right size load for the amount of clothes you have.

5. Select the right washing cycle. If your clothes are delicate, then select the delicate cycle.

6. Add the washing detergent.

7. Add fabric softener and bleach if you want. It is best to only use bleach on white clothing.

8. Close the door and press Start or Power to start the wash cycle.

9. When the wash cycle is finished, move your clothes to the dryer.

10. Select the right cycle on the dryer. Check the tag on your clothes, some say not to put them in the dryer.

1. Ask the students, "Who washes the clothes in your family?" (5 min).

2. Go through the routine (10 min).

3. Go through the routine again quickly and this time have the students record it on their phones (5 min).

4. As a class, role play the process of washing clothes, if possible, actually wash clothes in a real washing machine (15 min).

5. Describe an aspect of the setting, such as the washing machine, and have the students record the description on their phones, i.e. "The washing machine has a dispenser for the detergent, bleach and fabric softener. It has buttons for choosing temperature, size and washing cycle. It has a door which must be shut before you turn it on, etc."

6. Have the students take a photo of the setting to remind them of it when they are reviewing the routine for Homework later (5 min).

 STUDENTS TO LISTEN TO RECORDINGS WITH AN ENGLISH SPEAKER. TELL THEM TO STOP THE RECORDINGS IF THERE ARE ANY WORDS THEY DON'T UNDERSTAND FOR THE ENGLISH SPEAKER TO EXPLAIN (10 MIN).

Give Homework

 Give the students the Weekly Review Template and a copy of the pictures used in the lesson. Tell them to listen to their recordings and practice pointing to the correct pictures during the week. They should transcribe the recordings and try repeating what they hear. Remind them to bring the transcriptions to class for the next lesson for you to check for accuracy.

Washing Clothes

1. Sort your clothes into piles. It is best to wash clothes of the same color together, especially dark or light clothes.

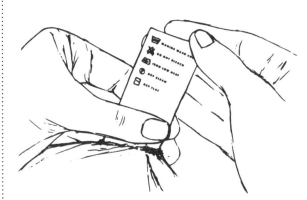

2. Read the 'care tag' on your clothes, it gives you information about your clothes.

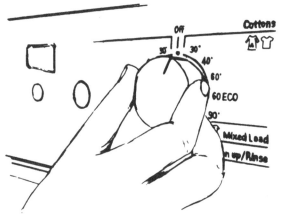

3. Set the right temperature. Hot water is best for dirty clothes, but cold water is best for dark colors so that the dye doesn't come out.

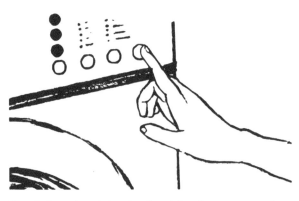

4. Select the right size load for the amount of clothes you have.

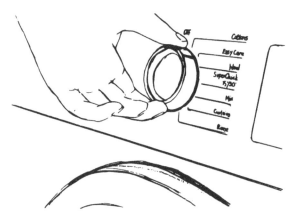

5. Select the right washing cycle. If your clothes are delicate, then select the delicate cycle.

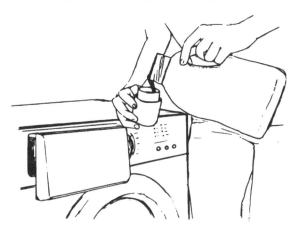

6. Add the washing detergent.

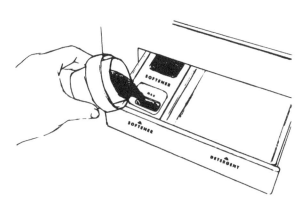

7   Add fabric softener and bleach if you want. It is best to only use bleach on white clothing.

8   Close the door and press Start or Power to start the wash cycle.

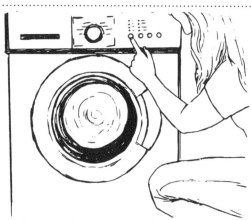

9   When the wash cycle is finished, move your clothes to the dryer.

10   Select the right cycle on the dryer. Check the tag on your clothes, some say not to put them in the dryer.

 ## Give Homework

 LISTEN TO YOUR RECORDING OF THE TEACHER GIVING THE STEPS FOR WASHING CLOTHES AND WRITE DOWN WHAT YOU HEAR.

Listen to the recording again and try repeating what you hear, sentence by sentence. See if you can also point to the correct pictures/perform the correct action as you repeat the recording. Remember to bring this to class with you next week!

....

....

....

....

Getting Ready

You will need
- Alarm clock
- Breakfast cereal
- Grooming items
- Handbag or backpack with things you need for the day
- Weekly Review Template
- Smartphone

Review

Recap last week's lesson and check students' homework activities (10 min).

Getting Ready in the Morning Routine

1. Set your alarm the night before.

2. Get up when the alarm goes off.

3. Take a shower.

4. Get dressed.

5. Brush your hair.

6. You might want to shave or put on makeup.

7. Eat breakfast.

8. Brush your teeth.

9. Gather the things you need for the day.

10. Get out the door! Try to leave a few minutes earlier than you need to.

1. Ask the students "How long does it take for you to get ready in the morning?" (5 min).

2. Go through the routine (10 min).

3. Go through the routine again quickly and this time have the students record it on their phones (5 min).

4. As a class or in pairs, role play the process of getting ready in the morning (15 min).

5. Describe an aspect of the setting, such as the shower, and have the students record the description on their phones, i.e. "The shower has a glass door. There are shampoo and conditioner bottles on the floor. It has a cold and hot water tap and a shower head. There is a shelf for soap and razors, etc." (5 min).

6. Have the students take a photo of the setting to remind them of it when they are reviewing the routine for Homework later (5 min).

 STUDENTS TO LISTEN TO RECORDINGS WITH AN ENGLISH SPEAKER. TELL THEM TO STOP THE RECORDINGS IF THERE ARE ANY WORDS THEY DON'T UNDERSTAND FOR THE ENGLISH SPEAKER TO EXPLAIN (10 MIN).

Give Homework

 Give the students the Weekly Review Template and a copy of the pictures used in the lesson. Tell them to listen to their recordings and practice pointing to the correct pictures during the week. They should transcribe the recordings and try repeating what they hear. Remind them to bring the transcriptions to class for the next lesson for you to check for accuracy.

Getting Ready

1. Set your alarm the night before.

2. Get up when the alarm goes off.

3. Take a shower.

4. Get dressed.

5. Brush your hair.

6. You might want to shave or put on makeup.

 Eat breakfast.

 Brush your teeth.

 Gather the things you need for the day.

 Get out the door!

✍ Give Homework

> 🗣)) LISTEN TO YOUR RECORDING OF THE TEACHER GIVING THE STEPS FOR GETTING READY AND WRITE DOWN WHAT YOU HEAR.

Listen to the recording again and try repeating what you hear, sentence by sentence. See if you can also point to the correct pictures/perform the correct action as you repeat the recording. Remember to bring this to class with you next week!

....

....

....

....

Shopping for Food

You will need
- Food items & shopping baskets
- Weekly Review Template
- Smartphone

Review

Recap last week's lesson and check students' homework activities (10 min).

Shopping Routine

1. Make a list.

2. Go to the store.

3. Get a shopping cart or basket.

4. Place items in your cart or basket as you shop.

    » Get fresh fruit and vegetables.

    » Ask for help at the deli counter.

    » Get baked goods as the bakery section.

    » Find grocery items in the aisles.

    » Go to the freezer and refrigerated sections.

5. Go to the checkout counter.

6. Place your items on the conveyor belt.

7. Leave empty baskets under the conveyor belt.

8. Provide your reusable bags to the cashier or bagger.

9. Provide any point cards and pay the casher.

10. Place your bags in the shopping cart. Remember to take the cart back when you're done.

1. Ask the students "Where do you go food shopping?" (5 min).

2. Go through the routine (10 min).

3. Go through the routine again quickly and this time have the students record it on their phones (5 min).

4. If possible, either role play shopping in class or take the class to a store to purchase some items (15 min).

5. Describe an aspect of the setting, such as the deli, and have the students record the description on their phones, i.e. "The deli has food inside glass cabinets. There is a section for cheese and a section for meat. There are people working behind the counter. They wear hats or nets on their heads and gloves on their hands to keep the food clean" (5 min).

6. Have the students take a photo of the setting to remind them of it when they are reviewing the routine for Homework later (5 min).

STUDENTS TO LISTEN TO RECORDINGS WITH AN ENGLISH SPEAKER. TELL THEM TO STOP THE RECORDINGS IF THERE ARE ANY WORDS THEY DON'T UNDERSTAND FOR THE ENGLISH SPEAKER TO EXPLAIN (10 MIN).

Give Homework

Give the students the Weekly Review Template and a copy of the pictures used in the lesson. Tell them to listen to their recordings and practice pointing to the correct pictures during the week. They should transcribe the recordings and try repeating what they hear. Remind them to bring the transcriptions to class for the next lesson for you to check for accuracy.

Shopping for Food

1 Make a list.

2 Go to the store.

3 Get a shopping cart or basket.

4 Place items in your cart or basket as you shop.

5 Go to the checkout counter.

6 Place your items on the conveyor belt.

7 Leave empty baskets under the conveyor belt.

8 Provide your reusable bags to the cashier or bagger.

9 Provide any point cards and pay the cashier.

10 Place your bags in the cart. Remember to take the cart back when you're done.

Give Homework

> LISTEN TO YOUR RECORDING OF THE TEACHER GIVING THE STEPS FOR GOING SHOPPING AND WRITE DOWN WHAT YOU HEAR.

Listen to the recording again and try repeating what you hear, sentence by sentence. See if you can also point to the correct pictures/perform the correct action as you repeat the recording. Remember to bring this to class with you next week!

Shopping for Clothes

You will need
- Shopping Bag
- Assortment of Clothes
- Weekly Review Template
- Smartphone

Review

Recap last week's lesson and check students' homework activities (10 min).

Shopping for Clothes Routine

1. Decide on a budget.

2. Decide which stores to visit based on what you need.

3. Wear clothes shopping that you can easily take off when trying on new clothes.

4. Pick out clothes you like. Be selective. Only pick clothes that look comfortable.

5. Look through the entire store.

6. Ask a salesperson for help if you want.

7. Choose clothes that are your size. Only buy the garment if it fits you now.

8. Try the clothes on.

   » Ask a salesperson if you can try the clothes on.

   » Go into the change room and try the clothes on.

9. Put the clothes you don't like back on the shelf.

10. Take the clothes you like to the counter and pay for them.

1. Ask the students "Where do you go shopping for clothes?" (5 min).

2. Go through the routine (10 min).

3. Go through the routine again quickly and this time have the students record it on their phones (5 min).

4. As a class, role play the process of shopping for clothes. (15 min).

5. Describe an aspect of setting and have the students record the description on their phones, i.e. "The clothing store has men's clothes on one side and women's clothes on the other. There is a counter near the front with a salesperson sitting behind it. There are some cubicles at the back for trying on clothes, etc." (5 min).

6. Have the students take a photo of the setting to remind them of it when they are reviewing the routine for Homework later (5 min).

STUDENTS TO LISTEN TO RECORDINGS WITH AN ENGLISH SPEAKER. TELL THEM TO STOP THE RECORDINGS IF THERE ARE ANY WORDS THEY DON'T UNDERSTAND FOR THE ENGLISH SPEAKER TO EXPLAIN (10 MIN).

Give Homework

Give the students the Weekly Review Template and a copy of the pictures used in the lesson. Tell them to listen to their recordings and practice pointing to the correct pictures during the week. They should transcribe the recordings and try repeating what they hear. Remind them to bring the transcriptions to class for the next lesson for you to check for accuracy.

Community Life ESL

Shopping for Clothes

1. Decide on a budget.

2. Decide which stores to visit based on what you need.

3. Wear clothes you can easily take off when shopping. You might want to try on some new clothes.

4. Pick out clothes you like.

5. Look through the entire store.

6. Ask a salesperson for help if you want.

 Choose clothes that are your size. Only buy garments that fit you now.

 Try the clothes on.
- Ask a salesperson if you can try the clothes on.
- Go into the change room and try the clothes on.

 Put the clothes you don't like back on the shelf.

 Take the clothes you like to the counter and pay for them.

Give Homework

> LISTEN TO YOUR RECORDING OF THE TEACHER GIVING THE STEPS FOR SHOPPING FOR CLOTHES AND WRITE DOWN WHAT YOU HEAR.

Listen to the recording again and try repeating what you hear, sentence by sentence. See if you can also point to the correct pictures/perform the correct action as you repeat the recording. Remember to bring this to class with you next week!

....

....

....

....

Using an ATM

You will need
- Debit Card
- Weekly Review Template
- Smartphone

Review

Recap last week's lesson and check students' homework activities (10 min).

Using an ATM Routine

1. Try to find an ATM that belongs to the same bank as your card. Then you will not have to pay a fee to withdraw money.

2. Make sure no one else is looking at your screen. This keeps your information safe.

3. Insert your card into the ATM.

4. Select your language.

5. Enter your PIN. PIN stands for Personal Identification Number. It's a password that allows you to access your bank account.

6. Withdraw money.

    » Choose the account type- Savings or Cheque.

    » Enter the amount you want to withdraw.

7. You can also check your account balance.

8. Follow the prompts to end your session when you are finished. Normally there is a cancel button.

9. Don't forget to take your card and money!

1. Ask the students "Who withdraws money from an ATM?" (5 min).

2. Go through the routine (10 min).

3. Go through the routine again quickly and this time have the students record it on their phones (5 min).

4. In pairs, have the students roleplay the routine (15 min).

5. Describe an aspect of setting and have the students record the description on their phones, i.e. "The ATM has a screen. It has a keypad with numbers and symbols. There is a place to insert your card and a place to take your money, etc." (5 min).

6. Have the students take a photo of the setting to remind them of it when they are reviewing the routine for Homework later (5 min).

STUDENTS TO LISTEN TO RECORDINGS WITH AN ENGLISH SPEAKER. TELL THEM TO STOP THE RECORDINGS IF THERE ARE ANY WORDS THEY DON'T UNDERSTAND FOR THE ENGLISH SPEAKER TO EXPLAIN (10 MIN).

Give Homework

Give the students the Weekly Review Template and a copy of the pictures used in the lesson. Tell them to listen to their recordings and practise pointing to the correct pictures during the week. They should transcribe the recordings and try repeating what they hear. Remind them to bring the transcriptions to class for the next lesson for you to check for accuracy.

Using an ATM

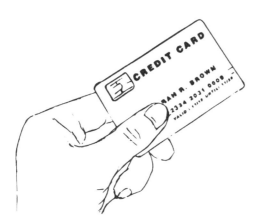

1 Try to find an ATM that belongs to the same bank as your card.

2 Make sure no one else is looking at your screen.

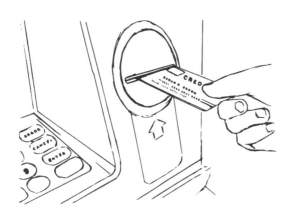

3 Insert your card into the ATM.

4 Select your language.

5 Enter your PIN.

6 Withdraw money.
 • Choose the account type - Savings or Cheque.
 • Enter the amount you want to withdraw.

7 You can also check your account balance.

8 Follow the prompts to end your session when you are finished.

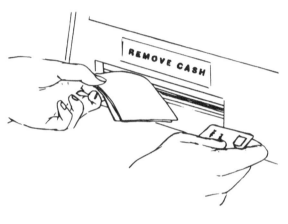

9 Don't forget to take your card and money!

 Give Homework

 LISTEN TO YOUR RECORDING OF THE TEACHER GIVING THE STEPS FOR USING AN ATM AND WRITE DOWN WHAT YOU HEAR.

Listen to the recording again and try repeating what you hear, sentence by sentence. See if you can also point to the correct pictures/perform the correct action as you repeat the recording. Remember to bring this to class with you next week!

....

....

....

....

Borrowing Books at the Library

You will need
- Library Card
- Books
- Weekly Review Template
- Smartphone

Review

Recap last week's lesson and check students' homework activities (10 min).

Borrowing Library Books Routine

1. Go to your local library.

2. Remember to talk quietly.

3. Go to the counter and ask for a library card.

4. Fill out the signup forms. Now you can borrow books!

5. Each section has different types of books. Go to the sections that interest you.

6. Pick out any books you like.

7. If you are looking for a particular book, search for it on a computer in the library.

   » Write down the location and number of the book to help you find it.

   » Look for the number on the spine of the book.

8. Ask a staff member if you need help finding a book.

9. Take your books to the counter and borrow them.

10. Make sure you bring the books back in time or you will be charged a fee!

1. Ask the students "Who has borrowed books at the library before?" (5 min).

2. Go through the routine (10 min).

3. Go through the routine again quickly and this time have the students record it on

their phones (5 min).

4. As a class, role play the process of borrowing a book at the library (15 min).

5. Describe an aspect of setting and have the students record the description on their phones, i.e. "The library has different sections for books. There is also a space for computers. You can use the computers to look for books. The staff members are putting the books away on the shelves, etc." (5 min).

6. Have the students take a photo of the setting to remind them of it when they are reviewing the routine for Homework later (5 min).

 STUDENTS TO LISTEN TO RECORDINGS WITH AN ENGLISH SPEAKER. TELL THEM TO STOP THE RECORDINGS IF THERE ARE ANY WORDS THEY DON'T UNDERSTAND FOR THE ENGLISH SPEAKER TO EXPLAIN (10 MIN).

Give Homework

 Give the students the Weekly Review Template and a copy of the pictures used in the lesson. Tell them to listen to their recordings and practice pointing to the correct pictures during the week. They should transcribe the recordings and try repeating what they hear. Remind them to bring the transcriptions to class for the next lesson for you to check for accuracy.

Borrowing Books at the Library

1. Go to your local library.

2. Remember to talk quietly.

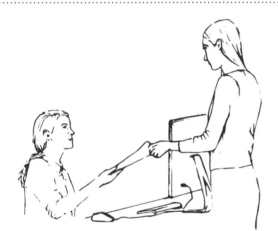

3. Go to the counter and ask for a library card.

4. Fill out the signup forms. Now you can borrow books!

5. Each section has different types of books. Go to the sections that interest you.

6. Pick out any books you like.

 If you are looking for a particular book, search for it on a computer in the library.

 Ask a staff member if you need help.

RETURNS

Take your books to the counter and borrow them.

Make sure you bring the books back in time or you will be charged a fee!

Give Homework

LISTEN TO YOUR RECORDING OF THE TEACHER GIVING THE STEPS FOR BORROWING BOOKS AND WRITE DOWN WHAT YOU HEAR.

Listen to the recording again and try repeating what you hear, sentence by sentence. See if you can also point to the correct pictures/perform the correct action as you repeat the recording. Remember to bring this to class with you next week!

....

....

....

....

Playing a Local Game

You will need
- Items needed for game, i.e. Bocce Ball set (or whatever game is common in your local area)
- Weekly Review Template
- Smartphone

Review

Recap last week's lesson and check students' homework activities (10 min).

Playing a Local Game Routine (i.e. Bocce Ball)

1. Get your bocce ball set. The set includes 8 balls and one smaller ball, called the jack.

2. Choose your teams. Bocce ball can be played either in teams against each other or as individuals against each other. Playing as individuals is suggested as scoring is easier.

3. Find an open space to play.

4. Decide who gets to throw the jack.

5. Throw the jack into the open space.

6. Take turns throwing the bocce balls. Get the ball as close to the jack as possible.

7. Measure which bocce ball is closest to the jack. The person/team who threw that ball is the winner!

1. Ask the students "What local games did you play in your town/village?" (5 min).

2. Go through the routine (10 min).

3. Go through the routine again quickly and this time have the students record it on their phones (5 min).

4. Play bocce ball as a class (15 min).

5. Describe the bocce ball set and have students record the description on their phones, i.e. "The bocce balls are in a metal case. There are 8 balls in the case. There is a small ball in the case. It is called the jack, etc." (5 min).

6. Have the students take a photo of the setting to remind them of it when they are reviewing the routine for Homework later (5 min).

STUDENTS TO LISTEN TO RECORDINGS WITH AN ENGLISH SPEAKER. TELL THEM TO STOP THE RECORDINGS IF THERE ARE ANY WORDS THEY DON'T UNDERSTAND FOR THE ENGLISH SPEAKER TO EXPLAIN (10 MIN).

Give Homework

Give the students the Weekly Review Template and a copy of the pictures used in the lesson. Tell them to listen to their recordings and practice pointing to the correct pictures during the week. They should transcribe the recordings and try repeating what they hear. Remind them to bring the transcriptions to class for the next lesson for you to check for accuracy.

Community Life ESL

Playing a Local Game

1. Get your bocce ball set. There are 8 balls and one smaller ball, called the jack.

2. Choose your teams.

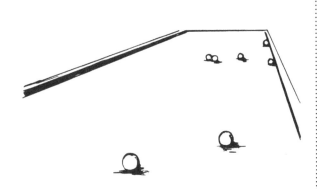

3. Find an open space to play.

4. Decide who gets to throw the jack.

5. Throw the jack into the open space.

6. Take turns throwing the bocce balls. Get the ball as close to the jack as possible.

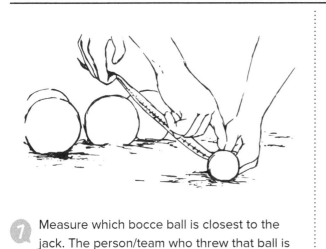

 Measure which bocce ball is closest to the jack. The person/team who threw that ball is the winner!

Give Homework

> LISTEN TO YOUR RECORDING OF THE TEACHER GIVING THE STEPS FOR PLAYING A LOCAL GAME AND WRITE DOWN WHAT YOU HEAR.

Listen to the recording again and try repeating what you hear, sentence by sentence. See if you can also point to the correct pictures/perform the correct action as you repeat the recording. Remember to bring this to class with you next week!

Getting a Haircut

You will need
- Magazines with pictures of hairstyles
- Hairdressing items such as scissors and an apron.
- Weekly Review Template
- Smartphone

Review

Recap last week's lesson and check students' homework activities (10 min).

Getting a Haircut Routine

1. Find a local hairdresser online. Men normally go to a barber while women normally go to a hairdresser or salon.

2. Make an appointment.

3. Bring a picture of the haircut you want.

4. Let the hairdresser or barber know you have arrived, i.e. "Hi I'm… and I'm here for my appointment".

5. Show the hairdresser or barber the picture of the haircut you want.

6. Tell them the name of the haircut you want if you know it.

7. Describe the length you want for your hair, i.e. a number 2 shave.

8. Be friendly. While the hairdresser or barber cuts your hair, you can talk to them. You can ask about their favorite tv shows and sports.

9. Ask about maintenance and upkeep for your new haircut.

10. When your haircut is finished, pay at the counter.

1. Ask the students "Where do you go to get your hair cut?" (5 min).

2. Go through the routine (10 min).

3. Go through the routine again quickly and this time have the students record it on their phones (5 min).

4. As a class or in pairs, role play the process of going to the hairdressers or barbers to get your hair cut (15 min).

5. Describe an aspect of the setting, such as the salon, and have the students record the description on their phones, i.e. "The hairdressing salon has mirrors on the wall. There are chairs in front of the mirrors. There are shelves with shampoo, hair dryers and scissors. There are pictures on the wall of different haircuts and styles" (5 min).

6. Have the students take a photo of the setting to remind them of it when they are reviewing the routine for Homework later (5 min).

 STUDENTS TO LISTEN TO RECORDINGS WITH AN ENGLISH SPEAKER. TELL THEM TO STOP THE RECORDINGS IF THERE ARE ANY WORDS THEY DON'T UNDERSTAND FOR THE ENGLISH SPEAKER TO EXPLAIN (10 MIN).

Give Homework

 Give the students the Weekly Review Template and a copy of the pictures used in the lesson. Tell them to listen to their recordings and practice pointing to the correct pictures during the week. They should transcribe the recordings and try repeating what they hear. Remind them to bring the transcriptions to class for the next lesson for you to check for accuracy.

Getting a Haircut

1 Find a local hairdresser online.

2 Make an appointment.

3 Bring a picture of the haircut you want.

4 Let the hairdresser or barber know you have arrived, i.e. "Hi I'm... and I'm here for my appointment".

5 Show them the picture of the haircut you want.

6 Tell them the name of the haircut you want, if you know it.

7 Describe the length you want for your hair.

8 Be friendly. While the hairdresser or barber cuts your hair, you can talk to them.

9 Ask about maintenance and upkeep for your new haircut.

10 When your haircut is finished, say "Thank you" and pay at the counter.

Give Homework

 LISTEN TO YOUR RECORDING OF THE TEACHER GIVING THE STEPS FOR GETTING A HAIRCUT AND WRITE DOWN WHAT YOU HEAR.

Listen to the recording again and try repeating what you hear, sentence by sentence. See if you can also point to the correct pictures/perform the correct action as you repeat the recording. Remember to bring this to class with you next week!

Going on a Bush Walk

You will need
- Bush walking items such as a map, water bottle, backpack, etc.
- Weekly Review Template
- Smartphone

Review

Recap last week's lesson and check students' homework activities (10 min).

Going on a Bush Walk Routine

1. Find local bush walking tracks online.

2. Start small. If it is your first time, pick a walk that is easy.

3. Pack your backpack. Don't forget to pack a map, phone, sun protection and lots of water.

4. Wear a hat and the right shoes.

5. Ask friends to go with you. If something difficult happens, they can help you.

6. Know what to do in case of an emergency. If you get lost, call emergency services and tell them name of the walk you are on, i.e. "I am lost somewhere on the 6 Foot Track in Katoomba".

7. Look for the signs.

8. Take breaks and rehydrate.

9. Look out for animals.

10. Take only pictures, leave only footprints. This is a saying that reminds us not to leave behind litter or take anything from nature.

1. Ask the students "Who has gone on a bush walk before?" (5 min).

2. Go through the routine (10 min).

3. Go through the routine again quickly and this time have the students record it on their phones (5 min).

4. As a class or in pairs, role play preparing to go on a bush walk, or actually go on a bush walk with class if possible (15 min).

5. Describe an aspect of the bush walk and have the students record the description on their phones, i.e. "The bush track is far away from houses. It is very long with trees on each side. There are some koalas in the trees. There are signs which show where to go, etc."

6. Have the students take a photo of the setting to remind them of it when they are reviewing the routine for Homework later (5 min).

STUDENTS TO LISTEN TO RECORDINGS WITH AN ENGLISH SPEAKER. TELL THEM TO STOP THE RECORDINGS IF THERE ARE ANY WORDS THEY DON'T UNDERSTAND FOR THE ENGLISH SPEAKER TO EXPLAIN (10 MIN).

Give Homework

Give the students the Weekly Review Template and a copy of the pictures used in the lesson. Tell them to listen to their recordings and practice pointing to the correct pictures during the week. They should transcribe the recordings and try repeating what they hear. Remind them to bring the transcriptions to class for the next lesson for you to check for accuracy.

 **Going on a Bush Walk**

1. Find local bush walking tracks online.

2. Start small. If it is your first time, pick a walk that is easy.

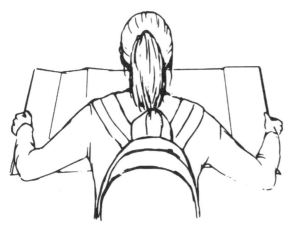

3. Pack your backpack. Don't forget a map, phone, sun protection and lots of water.

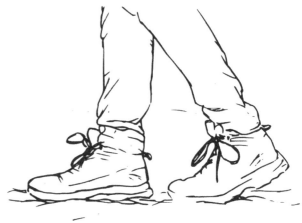

4. Wear a hat and the right shoes.

5. Ask friends to go with you. If something difficult happens, they can help you.

6. Know what to do in case of an emergency.

 Look for the signs.

 Look out for animals.

Take breaks and rehydrate.

Take only pictures, leave only footprints.

  Give Homework

> LISTEN TO YOUR RECORDING OF THE TEACHER GIVING THE STEPS FOR GOING ON A BUSH WALK AND WRITE DOWN WHAT YOU HEAR.

Listen to the recording again and try repeating what you hear, sentence by sentence. See if you can also point to the correct pictures/perform the correct action as you repeat the recording. Remember to bring this to class with you next week!

....

....

....

....

Going to the Beach

You will need
- Beach accessories, such as a swimsuit, sun protection, etc.
- Weekly Review Template
- Smartphone

Review

Recap last week's lesson and check students' homework activities (10 min).

Going to the Beach Routine

1. Pack everything you will need for the beach.

   » Swimsuit or board shorts, sun protection, change of clothes, water bottle, towel, sunglasses, hat, beach activities (ball, frisbee, bucket & spade, book), picnic basket, etc.

2. Read the beach signs.

3. Look for the red and yellow flags. This means that this is a safe place to swim. The life savers will protect you.

4. Swim between the flags. If there are no flags, don't swim.

5. It is best to swim with a friend. If you need help when you are swimming, then they can get the help you need.

6. If you hear a siren or bell sound, get out of the water.

7. If you need help, put your hand up so that the life savers can see you.

8. When you are finished swimming, you can take a shower at the bathrooms on the beach.

9. Dry yourself with a towel.

10. Enjoy doing some beach activities.

1. Ask the students "Who has gone to the beach?" and "What did you take?" (5 min).

2. Go through the routine (10 min).

3. Go through the routine again quickly and this time have the students record it on their phones (5 min).

4. Have the students discuss beach questions with helpers (15 min).

5. Describe the beach and have students record the description on their phones, i.e. "The beach is long and sandy. There are red and yellow flags at the beach and lots of people swimming, etc." (5 min).

6. Have the students take a photo of the setting to remind them of it when they are reviewing the routine for Homework later (5 min).

 STUDENTS TO LISTEN TO RECORDINGS WITH AN ENGLISH SPEAKER. TELL THEM TO STOP THE RECORDINGS IF THERE ARE ANY WORDS THEY DON'T UNDERSTAND FOR THE ENGLISH SPEAKER TO EXPLAIN (10 MIN).

Give Homework

 Give the students the Weekly Review Template and a copy of the pictures used in the lesson. Tell them to listen to their recordings and practice pointing to the correct pictures during the week. They should transcribe the recordings and try repeating what they hear. Remind them to bring the transcriptions to class for the next lesson for you to check for accuracy.

 # Going to the Beach

1 Pack everything you will need for the beach.

2 Read the beach signs.

3 Look for the red and yellow flags.

4 Swim between the flags (if there are no flags, don't swim).

5 It is best to swim with a friend.

6 If you hear a siren or bell sound, get out of the water.

7 If you need help, put your hand up so the life savers can see you.

8 When you are finished swimming, take a shower at the bathrooms on the beach.

9 Dry yourself with a towel.

10 Enjoy doing some beach activities.

Give Homework

 LISTEN TO YOUR RECORDING OF THE TEACHER GIVING THE STEPS FOR GOING TO THE BEACH AND WRITE DOWN WHAT YOU HEAR.

Listen to the recording again and try repeating what you hear, sentence by sentence. See if you can also point to the correct pictures/perform the correct action as you repeat the recording. Remember to bring this to class with you next week!

....

....

....

....

Making a Local Meal

You will need
- Ingredients for a local meal
- Weekly Review Template
- Smartphone

Review

Recap last week's lesson and check students' homework activities (10 min).

Lamington Recipe

Method	Ingredients

Method

1. Make icing. Sift the icing sugar and cocoa into a bowl.

2. Add butter and boiling water.

3. Stir the mixture until it is smooth.

4. Cut the sponge cake into 15 pieces.

5. Put the coconut in a dish.

6. Cover 1 piece of cake with the icing.

7. Cover the piece of cake with the coconut.

8. Put the iced cake on a tray.

9. Repeat with the remaining cake, dipping it into the icing and coconut.

10. Now you can eat!

Ingredients

1. 3 1/2 cups icing sugar

2. 1/4 cup cocoa powder

3. 1 tablespoon soft butter

4. 1/2 cup boiling water

5. Sponge cake (20cm x 30cm)

1. Give out a recipe from the local community (for example, in Australia it might be a lamington recipe).

2. Discuss new vocabulary "What are some words you can see on your recipe?"

   » Recipe - instructions for how to make a particular food, with a list of ingredients

   » Ingredients - food that are combined to make up a new food

   » Method - instructions that tell you how to do something

3. Go through the steps for making a local meal, i.e. lamingtons (or whatever meal is common in your local area) (10 min).

4. Go through the routine again quickly and have students record it on their phones (5 min).

5. Make the local meal as a class in a kitchen if possible (15 min).

6. Describe the local meal and have the students record the description on their phones, i.e. "The lamington is made from sponge cake. It is covered in chocolate and coconut. It is cut into a square shape. It is a traditional Australian recipe" (5 min).

7. Have the students take a photo of the setting to remind them of it when they are reviewing the routine for Homework later (5 min).

 STUDENTS TO LISTEN TO RECORDINGS WITH AN ENGLISH SPEAKER. TELL THEM TO STOP THE RECORDINGS IF THERE ARE ANY WORDS THEY DON'T UNDERSTAND FOR THE ENGLISH SPEAKER TO EXPLAIN (10 MIN).

Give Homework

 Give the students the Weekly Review Template and a copy of the pictures used in the lesson. Tell them to listen to their recordings and practice pointing to the correct pictures during the week. They should transcribe the recordings and try repeating what they hear. Remind them to bring the transcriptions to class for the next lesson for you to check for accuracy.

Making a Local Meal

1. Make icing.
   Sift icing sugar and cocoa into a bowl.

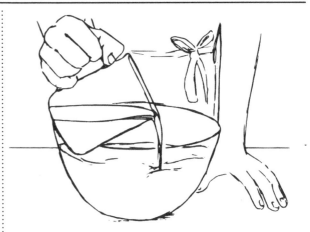

2. Add butter and boiling water.

3. Stir the mixture until it is smooth.

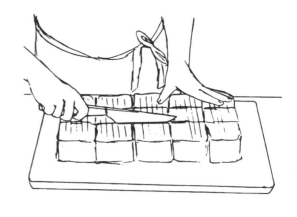

4. Cut the sponge cake into 15 pieces.

5. Cover 1 piece of cake with the icing.

6. Put the coconut in a dish.

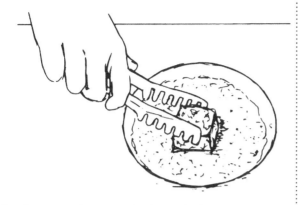

 Cover each piece of cake with the coconut.

8 Put the iced cake on a tray.

 Repeat with the remaining cake, dipping it into the icing and coconut.

10 Now you can eat!

Lamington Recipe

Method

1. Make icing. Sift icing sugar and cocoa into a bowl.
2. Add butter and boiling water.
3. Stir the mixture until it is smooth.
4. Cut sponge cake into 15 pieces.
5. Put coconut in a dish.
6. Cover 1 piece of cake with icing.
7. Cover each piece of cake with coconut.
8. Put the iced cake on a tray.
9. Repeat with remaining cake, dipping it into the icing and coconut.
10. Now you can eat!

Ingredients

1. 3 1/2 cups icing sugar
2. 1/4 cup cocoa powder
3. 1 tablespoon soft butter
4. 1/2 cup boiling water
5. Sponge cake (20cm x 30cm)

Give Homework

>  LISTEN TO YOUR RECORDING OF THE TEACHER GIVING THE STEPS FOR MAKING A LOCAL MEAL AND WRITE DOWN WHAT YOU HEAR.

Listen to the recording again and try repeating what you hear, sentence by sentence. See if you can also point to the correct pictures/perform the correct action as you repeat the recording. Remember to bring this to class with you next week!

....

....

....

....

....

....

....

....

....

....

....

....

....

....

Attending a Sports Game

You will need
- Tickets to the game
- Weekly Review Template
- Smartphone

Review

Recap last week's lesson and check students' homework activities (10 min).

Attending a Sports Game Routine

1. Go online and check the dates for the team that you want to see play.

2. Buy tickets to the game. Some community games are free to attend.

3. Travel to the stadium or sports field.

4. Go through security. You will have to show your ticket to the security guard and at some stadiums they will also search your bags.

5. Find your seats. At large stadiums an attendant will look at your ticket and show you where your seats are.

6. Watch the game. Many games have apps online where you can look up the players and the teams.

7. Check the scoreboard to keep track of the score.

8. During halftime you can go to buy some snacks or use the bathroom.

9. After the game is over, leave the stadium. You might like to buy some team merchandise like a hat or a scarf on your way out.

10. Travel home.

1. Ask the students "What sports game did you go to?" (5 min).

2. Go through the routine (10 min).

3. Go through the routine again quickly and this time have the students record it on their phones (5 min).

4. As a class or in pairs, role play the process of attending a sports game (15 min).

5. Describe an aspect of the setting, such as the stadium, and have the students record the description on their phones, i.e. "The stadium has four different stands; all the stands have different names. One of the stands was very old while the other three were much more modern. The stadium has two levels with seats that slope down towards the field, etc." (5 min).

6. Have the students take a photo of the setting to remind them of it when they are reviewing the routine for Homework later (5 min).

STUDENTS TO LISTEN TO RECORDINGS WITH AN ENGLISH SPEAKER. TELL THEM TO STOP THE RECORDINGS IF THERE ARE ANY WORDS THEY DON'T UNDERSTAND FOR THE ENGLISH SPEAKER TO EXPLAIN (10 MIN).

Give Homework

Give the students the Weekly Review Template and a copy of the pictures used in the lesson. Tell them to listen to their recordings and practice pointing to the correct pictures during the week. They should transcribe the recordings and try repeating what they hear. Remind them to bring the transcriptions to class for the next lesson for you to check for accuracy.

Community Life ESL

Attending a Sports Game

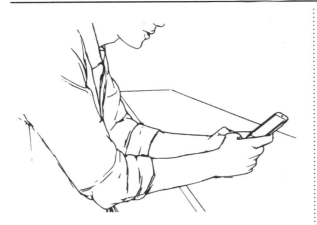

1 Go online and check the dates for the team that you want to see play.

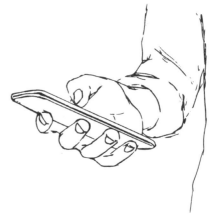

2 Buy tickets to the game. Some community games are free to attend.

3 Travel to the stadium or sports field.

4 Go through security. You will have to show your ticket to the security guard and at some stadiums they will also search your bags.

5 Find your seats. At large stadiums an attendant will look at your ticket and show you where your seats are.

6 Watch the game. Many games have apps online where you can look up the players and the teams.

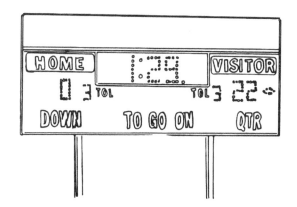

 Check the scoreboard to keep track of the score.

During halftime you can go to buy some snacks or use the bathroom.

 After the game is over, leave the stadium. You might like to buy some team merchandise like a hat or a scarf on your way out.

Travel home.

 Give Homework

> LISTEN TO YOUR RECORDING OF THE TEACHER GIVING THE STEPS FOR ATTENDING A SPORTS GAME AND WRITE DOWN WHAT YOU HEAR.

Listen to the recording again and try repeating what you hear, sentence by sentence. See if you can also point to the correct pictures/perform the correct action as you repeat the recording. Remember to bring this to class with you next week!

Attending a Church Service

You will need
- Bibles and other items in a church service, i.e. bulletins, etc.
- Weekly Review Template
- Smartphone

Review

Recap last week's lesson and check students' homework activities (10 min).

Attending a Church Service Routine

1. You might want to bring a friend with you.

2. Arrive a few minutes early.

3. Try to talk to some members. Tell them that you are new.

4. Sit down in a seat next to other people.

5. Follow the lead of others. If they stand to sing, you can stand too. Don't worry if you don't know the words!

6. Listen to the Bible talk. When the pastor reads from the Bible, the words might be on the screen. Or if there is a Bible near you, you can open it and read the same passage the pastor is reading.

7. When the service is finished, say hello to the people sitting near you.

8. Don't be afraid to ask questions.

9. If there are some snacks and tea or coffee, you can get some.

10. When you are ready to go, you can say "Goodbye, see you later!"

1. Ask the students "Who has been to a church service? What did you do when you went?" (5 min).

2. Go through the routine (10 min).

3. Go through the routine again quickly and this time have the students record it on their phones (5 min).

4. Role play the process of attending a church service as a class (15 min).

5. Describe an aspect of the church service and have the students record the description on their phones, i.e. "The church building has lots of rooms. There is a big room where everyone sits together. There is a kitchen with tea and coffee. There is a smaller room with toys and books for children, etc." (5 min).

6. Have the students take a photo of the setting to remind them of it when they are reviewing the routine for Homework later (5 min).

> STUDENTS TO LISTEN TO RECORDINGS WITH AN ENGLISH SPEAKER. TELL THEM TO STOP THE RECORDINGS IF THERE ARE ANY WORDS THEY DON'T UNDERSTAND FOR THE ENGLISH SPEAKER TO EXPLAIN (10 MIN).

Give Homework

Give the students the Weekly Review Template and a copy of the pictures used in the lesson. Tell them to listen to their recordings and practice pointing to the correct pictures during the week. They should transcribe the recordings and try repeating what they hear. Remind them to bring the transcriptions to class for the next lesson for you to check for accuracy.

Attending a Church Service

1 It might be nice to bring a friend.

2 Arrive a few minutes early.

3 Try to talk to some members. Tell them that you are new.

4 Sit down in a seat next to other people.

5 Follow the lead of others. If they stand to sing, you can stand too.

6 Listen to the Bible talk.

7 When the service is finished, say hello to the people near you.

8 Don't be afraid to ask questions.

9 If there are snacks and tea or coffee, you can get some.

10 When you are ready to go, you can say "Goodbye, see you later".

 Give Homework

LISTEN TO YOUR RECORDING OF THE TEACHER GIVING THE STEPS FOR ATTENDING A CHURCH AND WRITE DOWN WHAT YOU HEAR.

Listen to the recording again and try repeating what you hear, sentence by sentence. See if you can also point to the correct pictures/perform the correct action as you repeat the recording. Remember to bring this to class with you next week!

....

....

....

....

Attending a Bible Study

You will need
- Bible study guide
- Bible
- Pen
- Notebook
- Weekly Review Template
- Smartphone

Review

Recap last week's lesson and check students' homework activities (10 min).

Attending a Bible Study Routine

1. Prepare for the study by reading over the Bible passage.

2. Pack a Bible, a pen, and a notebook.

3. When you arrive, say hello to everyone. You might have a snack together.

4. Read the Bible passage together.

5. Think about the discussion questions that the leader gives.

6. Answer some questions if you would like.

7. At the end, the leader might ask for prayer requests.

8. You can listen to people as they pray.

9. When you are ready to leave, say goodbye.

1. Ask the students "Who has gone to a Bible study before?" (5 min).

2. Go through the routine (10 min).

3. Go through the routine again quickly and this time have the students record it on their phones (5 min).

4. As a class, role play the process of attending a Bible study (15 min).

5. Describe an aspect of the setting, such as the Bible study guide, and have the students record the description on their phones, i.e. "The Bible study guide has 10 studies. Each study has a Bible passage to read and discussion questions to talk about. There is a place to take notes, etc." (5 min).

6. Have the students take a photo of the setting to remind them of it when they are reviewing the routine for Homework later (5 min).

STUDENTS TO LISTEN TO RECORDINGS WITH AN ENGLISH SPEAKER. TELL THEM TO STOP THE RECORDINGS IF THERE ARE ANY WORDS THEY DON'T UNDERSTAND FOR THE ENGLISH SPEAKER TO EXPLAIN (10 MIN).

Give Homework

Give the students the Weekly Review Template and a copy of the pictures used in the lesson. Tell them to listen to their recordings and practice pointing to the correct pictures during the week. They should transcribe the recordings and try repeating what they hear. Remind them to bring the transcriptions to class for the next lesson for you to check for accuracy.

Attending a Bible Study

1. Prepare for the study by reading over the Bible passage.

2. Pack your Bible, a pen, and a notebook.

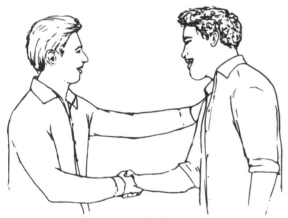

3. When you arrive, say hello to everyone. You might have a snack together.

4. Read the Bible passage together.

5. Think about the discussion questions that the leader gives.

6. Answer some questions if you would like.

 At the end, the leader might ask for prayer requests.

 You can listen to people as they pray.

 When you are ready to leave, say goodbye.

Give Homework

> LISTEN TO YOUR RECORDING OF THE TEACHER GIVING THE STEPS FOR ATTENDING A BIBLE STUDY AND WRITE DOWN WHAT YOU HEAR.

Listen to the recording again and try repeating what you hear, sentence by sentence. See if you can also point to the correct pictures/perform the correct action as you repeat the recording. Remember to bring this to class with you next week!

Going to the Movies

You will need
- Movie ticket
- Movie snacks
- DVDs
- Weekly Review Template
- Smartphone

Review

Recap last week's lesson and check students' homework activities (10 min).

Going to the Movies Routine

1. Decide what movie to see.

2. Buy the tickets online or at the box office.

3. Arrive early so you will get a good seat.

4. Buy snacks and drinks if you want.

5. Pick your seats. Your seat number might be on your ticket. If not, you can pick your own seat.

6. Watch the movie quietly.

7. If you want to talk about the movie, talk about it with friends afterwards.

8. Put your litter in the bin as you walk out.

1. Ask the students "What is your favorite movie?" (5 min).

2. Go through the routine (10 min).

3. Go through the routine again quickly and this time have the students record it on their phones (5 min).

4. As a class, role play the process of going to the movies, or actually go to the movies as a class if possible (15 min)

5. Describe an aspect of the setting, such as the cinema, and have the students record the description on their phones, i.e. "The cinema has several theaters where they play different movies. There is a snack shop with popcorn, icecream and drinks. There is a screen above the box office showing all the different movies you can choose from, etc." (5 min).

6. Have the students take a photo of the setting to remind them of it when they are reviewing the routine for Homework later (5 min).

 STUDENTS TO LISTEN TO RECORDINGS WITH AN ENGLISH SPEAKER. TELL THEM TO STOP THE RECORDINGS IF THERE ARE ANY WORDS THEY DON'T UNDERSTAND FOR THE ENGLISH SPEAKER TO EXPLAIN (10 MIN).

Give Homework

 Give the students the Weekly Review Template and a copy of the pictures used in the lesson. Tell them to listen to their recordings and practice pointing to the correct pictures during the week. They should transcribe the recordings and try repeating what they hear. Remind them to bring the transcriptions to class for the next lesson for you to check for accuracy.

Community Life ESL Going to the Movies

1 Decide what movie to see.

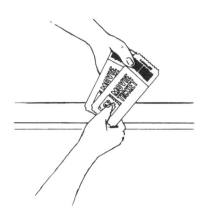

2 Buy the tickets online or at the box office.

3 Arrive early so you will get a good seat.

4 Buy snacks and drinks if you want.

5 Pick your seats. Your seat number might be on your ticket. If not, you can pick your own seat.

6 Watch the movie quietly.

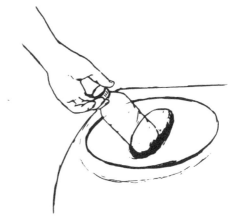

7 If you want to talk about the movie, talk about it with friends afterwards.

8 Put your litter in the bin as you walk out.

 ## Give Homework

 LISTEN TO YOUR RECORDING OF THE TEACHER GIVING THE STEPS FOR GOING TO THE MOVIES AND WRITE DOWN WHAT YOU HEAR.

Listen to the recording again and try repeating what you hear, sentence by sentence. See if you can also point to the correct pictures/perform the correct action as you repeat the recording. Remember to bring this to class with you next week!

....

....

....

....

....

....

....

....

....

Looking after a Pet

You will need
- Pet and pet accessories (or pictures of them)
- Weekly Review Template
- Smartphone

Review

Recap last week's lesson and check students' homework activities (10 min).

Looking after a Pet Routine

1. Make sure you have everything your pet will need. If it is a dog, this includes things such as a dog bed, dog bowls for food and water, dog food, and a leash and collar.

2. Take your pet to the vet if it is sick. If it is a puppy, it will need to have its vaccinations.

3. Spend time with your pet.

4. Provide a place for your pet to sleep.

5. Feed your pet every day. Provide fresh water at all times. Feed your pet the right kind of food so it has a healthy diet.

6. Give your pet exercise, if you have a dog you can take it for walks.

7. Groom and wash your pet.

8. Train your pet carefully and consistently. Always reward your pet, with a treat or a pat, when it has done something well during training.

9. Have someone look after your pet when you're away.

1. Ask the students "Who has a pet?" Or "What kinds of pets have you had in the past?" (5 min).

2. Using a real pet, go through the routine, where possible demonstrating steps (20 min).

3. Go through the routine again quickly and this time have the students record it on their phones (5 min).

4. Describe the pet and have the students record the description on their phones, i.e. "The dog is brown, with a white spot on her chest. She is a sausage dog, so she has a long body, long ears and short legs. She is a puppy, so she is very playful" (5 min).

5. Have the students take a photo of the setting to remind them of it when they are reviewing the routine for Homework later (5 min).

STUDENTS TO LISTEN TO RECORDINGS WITH AN ENGLISH SPEAKER. TELL THEM TO STOP THE RECORDINGS IF THERE ARE ANY WORDS THEY DON'T UNDERSTAND FOR THE ENGLISH SPEAKER TO EXPLAIN (10 MIN).

Give Homework

Give the students the Weekly Review Template and a copy of the pictures used in the lesson. Tell them to listen to their recordings and practice pointing to the correct pictures during the week. They should transcribe the recordings and try repeating what they hear. Remind them to bring the transcriptions to class for the next lesson for you to check for accuracy.

Community Life ESL — Looking after a Pet

1 Find the right kind of dog for you.

2 Make sure you have everything your dog will need.

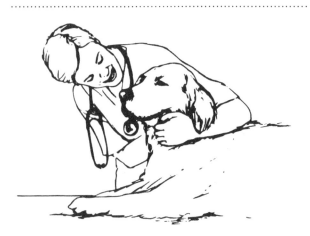

3 Take your dog to the vet if it is sick or if it needs vaccinations.

4 Spend time with your dog.

5 Provide a place for your dog to sleep.

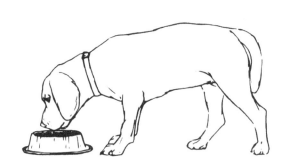

6 Feed your dog.

7 Take your dog for walks.

8 Groom and wash your dog.

9 Train your dog carefully and consistently.

10 Have someone look after your dog when you're gone.

Give Homework

 LISTEN TO YOUR RECORDING OF THE TEACHER GIVING THE STEPS FOR LOOKING AFTER A PET AND WRITE DOWN WHAT YOU HEAR.

Listen to the recording again and try repeating what you hear, sentence by sentence. See if you can also point to the correct pictures/perform the correct action as you repeat the recording. Remember to bring this to class with you next week!

....

....

....

....

Having a BBQ

You will need
- BBQ and items such as BBQ utensils (or pictures of them)
- Weekly Review Template
- Smartphone

Review

Recap last week's lesson and check students' homework activities (10 min).

Having a BBQ Routine

1. Prepare the meat and vegetables for cooking. You may want to marinate them.

2. Turn on the BBQ. Either turn on the gas or put coals in the bottom and light.

3. Wait 10-20 minutes for the BBQ to heat up.

4. Clean the hot plates. Scrape off any food and wash with water.

5. Spray oil on the BBQ.

6. Place the meat and vegetables on the BBQ.

7. Turn the meat and vegetables using a spatula or tongs.

8. Remove the meat and vegetables when they are cooked on both sides.

9. Clean the hot plates again. Scrape off any food and wash with water.

10. Now you can eat! You may want to have salad and bread rolls with your BBQ.

1. Ask the students "Who has had a BBQ recently?" (5 min).

2. Go through the routine (10 min).

3. Go through the routine again quickly and this time have the students record it on their phones (5 min).

4. Have a BBQ as a class as an end of term activity. If not possible, role play the process as a class (15 min).

5. Describe an aspect of the setting, such as the BBQ, and have the students record the description on their phones, i.e. "The BBQ has a hot plate and a grill. There is a knob to turn it on. It is on wheels, so it is easy to move. It also has a lid, etc." (5 min).

6. Have the students take a photo of the setting to remind them of it when they are reviewing the routine for Homework later (5 min).

 STUDENTS TO LISTEN TO RECORDINGS WITH AN ENGLISH SPEAKER. TELL THEM TO STOP THE RECORDINGS IF THERE ARE ANY WORDS THEY DON'T UNDERSTAND FOR THE ENGLISH SPEAKER TO EXPLAIN (10 MIN).

Give Homework

 Give the students the Weekly Review Template and a copy of the pictures used in the lesson. Tell them to listen to their recordings and practice pointing to the correct pictures during the week. They should transcribe the recordings and try repeating what they hear. Remind them to bring the transcriptions to class for the next lesson for you to check for accuracy.

Having a BBQ

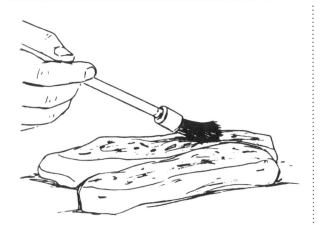

1 Prepare the meat and vegetables for cooking. You may want to marinate them.

2 Turn on the BBQ. Either turn on the gas or put coals in the bottom and light.

3 Wait 10-20 minutes for the BBQ to heat up.

4 Clean the BBQ. Scrape off any food and wash with water.

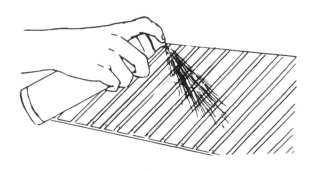

5 Spray oil on the BBQ.

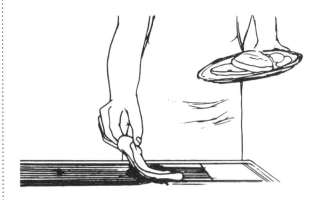

6 Place the meat and vegetable on the BBQ.

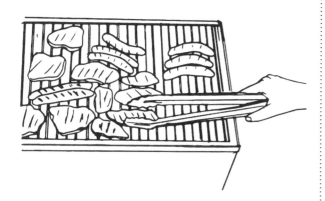

 7 Turn the meat and vegetables using a spatula or tongs.

8 Remove the vegetables using a spatula or tongs.

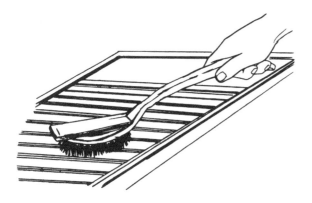

 9 Clean the BBQ again. Scrape off any food and wash with water.

10 Now you can eat! You may want to have salad and bread rolls with your BBQ.

Give Homework

 LISTEN TO YOUR RECORDING OF THE TEACHER GIVING THE STEPS FOR HAVING A BBQ AND WRITE DOWN WHAT YOU HEAR.

Listen to the recording again and try repeating what you hear, sentence by sentence. See if you can also point to the correct pictures/perform the correct action as you repeat the recording. Remember to bring this to class with you next week!

....

....

....

....

Mowing the Grass

You will need
- Lawn mower & accessories (or pictures of them)
- Weekly Review Template
- Smartphone

Review

Recap last week's lesson and check students' homework activities (10 min).

Mowing the Grass Routine

1. Wear the right clothes and protection.

2. Move the lawn mower to an open, grassy area. Clear away any objects in the way.

3. Check the lawn mower has fuel. If the fuel is low, pour fuel into the tank.

4. Set your mower to the right height (between 5-7 cm).

5. Prime the carburetor.

    » To do this, push the prime button 3 or 4 times. The prime button is usually a red or black squishy button somewhere on the mower.

6. Open the throttle.

    » There will usually be a lever on the handle of the lawnmower or somewhere on the engine. Put the throttle lever in a high position.

7. Pull the starter cord.

    » Hold the handle of the starter, attached at the end of a rope or cord, and pull upward quickly and firmly. You may have to do this several times before the motor starts up.

8. Push the lawn mower in straight lines over the grass.

9. When you are finished mowing, stop the lawn mower by closing the throttle. You can do this by pushing the lever back to a low position.

1. Ask the students "Who mows the grass at your house?" (5 min).

2. Go through the routine (10 min).

3. Go through the routine again quickly and this time have the students record it on their phones (5 min).

4. Go outside and demonstrate starting the lawn mower and mowing grass (15 min).

5. Describe the lawn mower and have the students record the description on their phones, i.e. "The lawn mower has a starter cord. The starter cord has a handle. The handle is red, etc." (5 min).

6. Have the students take a photo of the setting to remind them of it when they are reviewing the routine for Homework later (5 min).

 STUDENTS TO LISTEN TO BOTH RECORDINGS WITH A HELPER. TELL THEM TO STOP THE RECORDINGS IF THERE ARE ANY WORDS THEY DON'T UNDERSTAND FOR HELPER TO EXPLAIN (10 MIN).

Give Homework

 Give the students the Weekly Review Template and a copy of the pictures used in the lesson. Tell them to listen to their recordings and practice pointing to the correct pictures during the week. They should transcribe the recordings and try repeating what they hear. Remind them to bring the transcriptions to class for the next lesson for you to check for accuracy.

Mowing the Grass

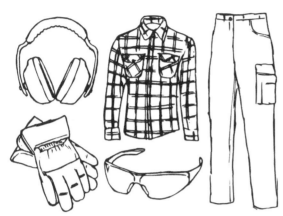

1. Wear the right clothes and protection.

2. Move the lawn mower to an open, grassy area. Clear away any objects in the way.

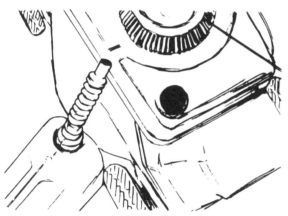

3. Check the lawn mower has fuel.

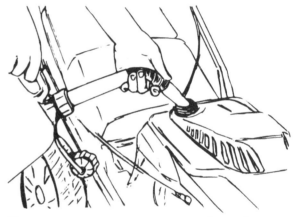

4. If the fuel is low, pour fuel into the tank.

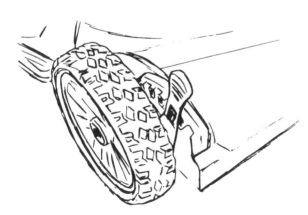

5. Set your mower to the right height (between 5-7cm).

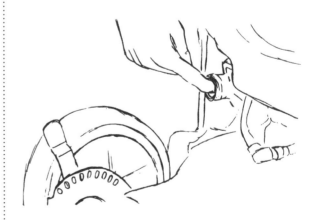

6. Prime the carburetor. Press the prime button 3 or 4 times.

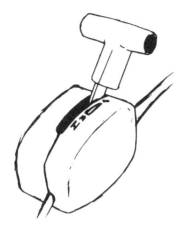

7 Open the throttle. Put the throttle lever in high position.

8 Pull the starter cord. Hold the handle of the starter and pull upward quickly and firmly.

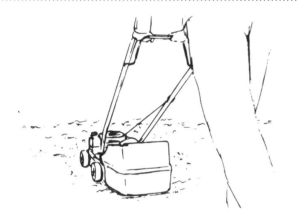

9 Push the lawn mower in straight lines over the grass.

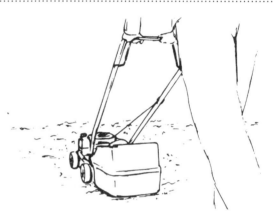

10 When you are finished, stop the lawn mower by closing the throttle. You can do this by pushing the lever back to a low position.

Give Homework

 LISTEN TO YOUR RECORDING OF THE TEACHER GIVING THE STEPS FOR MOWING THE GRASS AND WRITE DOWN WHAT YOU HEAR.

Listen to the recording again and try repeating what you hear, sentence by sentence. See if you can also point to the correct pictures/perform the correct action as you repeat the recording. Remember to bring this to class with you next week!

....

....

....

....

Potting a Plant

You will need
- Plant and potting items, such as a pot, soil, gloves, etc.
- Weekly Review Template
- Smartphone

Review

Recap last week's lesson and check students' homework activities (10 min).

Potting a Plant Routine

1. Choose a pot with drainage holes that is the right size for your plant.

2. Fill the bottom third of the pot with rocks or gravel to help with drainage.

3. Add potting soil up to 5 cm below the rim of the pot.

4. Add plant food and nutrients.

5. Water the plant and take it carefully out of its container. Squeeze the sides of the container, don't pull the plant.

6. Massage the roots gently.

7. Dig a hole for the plant.

8. Place the plant in the hole and cover with soil.

9. Place a saucer underneath to catch the water.

10. Water the plant regularly.

1. Ask the students "Who has potted a plant before?" (5 min).

2. Go through the routine (10 min).

3. Go through the routine again quickly and this time have the students record it on their phones (5 min).

4. As a class, role play the process of potting a plant (15 min).

5. Describe an aspect of the setting, such as the pot, and have the students record the description on their phones, i.e. "The pot has holes in the bottom that let the water out. It is made from plastic. It has a saucer underneath to catch water, etc." (5 min).

6. Have the students take a photo of the setting to remind them of it when they are reviewing the routine for Homework later (5 min).

STUDENTS TO LISTEN TO RECORDINGS WITH AN ENGLISH SPEAKER. TELL THEM TO STOP THE RECORDINGS IF THERE ARE ANY WORDS THEY DON'T UNDERSTAND FOR THE ENGLISH SPEAKER TO EXPLAIN (10 MIN).

Give Homework

Give the students the Weekly Review Template and a copy of the pictures used in the lesson. Tell them to listen to their recordings and practice pointing to the correct pictures during the week. They should transcribe the recordings and try repeating what they hear. Remind them to bring the transcriptions to class for the next lesson for you to check for accuracy.

Potting a Plant

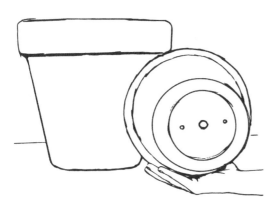

1 Choose a pot with drainage holes that is the right size for your plant.

2 Fill the bottom third of the pot with rocks or gravel to help with drainage.

3 Add potting soil up to 5 cm below the rim of the pot.

4 Add plant food and nutrients.

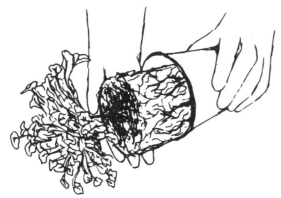

5 Water the plant and carefully take it out of its container. Squeeze the sides of the container, don't pull the plant.

6 Massage the roots gently.

7 Dig a hole for the plant.

8 Place the plant in the hole and cover with soil.

9 Place a saucer underneath the pot to catch the water.

10 Water the plant regularly.

Give Homework

 LISTEN TO YOUR RECORDING OF THE TEACHER GIVING THE STEPS FOR POTTING A PLANT AND WRITE DOWN WHAT YOU HEAR.

Listen to the recording again and try repeating what you hear, sentence by sentence. See if you can also point to the correct pictures/perform the correct action as you repeat the recording. Remember to bring this to class with you next week!

....

....

....

....

Ordering Pizza

You will need
- Cash for pizza
- Weekly Review Template
- Smartphone

Review

Recap last week's lesson and check students' homework activities (10 min).

Ordering Pizza Routine

1. Search the internet for 'pizza shops'.

2. Pick your local pizza shop and look at the menu.

3. Decide what to order. Call the number.

4. Order food, i.e. "Hi, I'd like to order 2 pizzas". Give them your address.

5. Organise payment. You can usually pay with your credit card or pay the driver with cash.

6. Open the door when you hear a knock.

7. Pay the driver when he or she gives you the pizza, if you haven't already. Thank them and say goodbye.

1. Go through the routine (10 min).

2. Go through the routine again quickly and this time have the students record it on their phones (5 min).

3. Model ordering pizza on the phone with one of the English helpers. An example script is provided below.

4. Order pizza as a class (if possible). Have one student volunteer to go through all the steps (10 min).

5. While you wait for the pizza to arrive, have students role play the routine with helpers, taking turns being the customer and staff (10 min).

6. Describe the pizza and have the students record the description on their phones, i.e. "The pizza has a thin crust. It has tomato sauce, cheese, pineapple and ham as the toppings. It is cut into six pieces. It comes in a cardboard box. The box keeps it warm, etc." (5 min).

7. When the pizza arrives, enjoy eating it together as a class. Have the students take a photo of the setting to remind them of it when they are reviewing the routine for Homework later (5 min).

STUDENTS TO LISTEN TO RECORDINGS WITH AN ENGLISH SPEAKER. TELL THEM TO STOP THE RECORDINGS IF THERE ARE ANY WORDS THEY DON'T UNDERSTAND FOR THE ENGLISH SPEAKER TO EXPLAIN (10 MIN).

Give Homework

Give the students the Weekly Review Template and a copy of the pictures used in the lesson. Tell them to listen to their recordings and practice pointing to the correct pictures during the week. They should transcribe the recordings and try repeating what they hear. Remind them to bring the transcriptions to class for the next lesson for you to check for accuracy.

Ordering the Pizza on the Phone Script

Customer: *Hi I'd like to order two pizzas for delivery. One Margherita and one Pepperoni.*

Staff: *Sure, can I get you anything else?*

Customer: *No, that's all thanks*

Staff: *When would you like that delivered?*

Customer: *7:30pm please*

Staff: *What's your address?*

Customer: *The address is the address is Country Church. We're on 100 North Street, Springwood. We can meet you at the front of the church.*

Staff: *Okay, that will be $15.50. How would you like to pay?*

Customer: *We'll pay the driver in cash.*

Staff: *Great, we'll see you soon.*

Customer: *Thanks. Bye.*

1. Search on the internet for 'pizza shops'.

2. Pick your local pizza shop and look at the menu.

3. Decide what to order. Call the number.

4. Order food, i.e. "Hi, I'd like to order 2 pizzas". Give them your address.

5. Organise payment. You can usually pay with your credit card or pay the driver in cash.

6. Open the door when you hear a knock.

 Pay the driver when he gives you the pizza. Thank them and say goodbye.

 Give Homework

> LISTEN TO YOUR RECORDING OF THE TEACHER GIVING THE STEPS FOR ORDERING PIZZA AND WRITE DOWN WHAT YOU HEAR.

Listen to the recording again and try repeating what you hear, sentence by sentence. See if you can also point to the correct pictures/perform the correct action as you repeat the recording. Remember to bring this to class with you next week!

....

....

....

....

....

....

....

....

....

Riding a Bike

You will need
- Bike and bike accessories (or pictures of them)
- Weekly Review Template
- Smartphone

Review

Recap last week's lesson and check students' homework activities (10 min).

Riding a Bike Routine

1. Wear riding clothing. Sports shoes and trousers are good to wear (don't wear skirts or baggy pants, as they may get caught in the tires).

2. Find a flat location to ride, away from traffic.

3. Put on a helmet.

4. Adjust the bike seat, you should have both of your feet flat on the ground when seated.

5. Test the brakes.

6. Start with one foot on the ground.

7. Start gliding.

   » Rather than pedal, push yourself off with your foot. Tuck your feet upwards and onto the pedals.

8. Start pedaling. Keep going as long as you can maintain balance.

9. Look straight ahead.

   » Don't look at obstacles or you might steer towards them accidentally. Look the way you want your bike to go.

10. Dismount the bike.

    » Use the brakes to stop, not your foot. Stop pedaling and squeeze both handbrakes. Once the bike has stopped, step off onto the ground.

1. Ask the students "Who knows how to ride a bike?" or "Who taught you how to ride?" (5 min).

2. Go through the routine (10 min).

3. Go through the routine again quickly and this time have the students record it on their phones (5 min).

4. Model to the students how to ride a bike, going through the routine for real (if possible). Have the students try (15 min).

5. Describe the bike and have the students record the description on their phones, i.e. "The bike has wheels, pedals and brakes. It has a seat and a horn. You have to adjust the seat to the right height, etc." (5 min).

6. Have the students take a photo of the setting to remind them of it when they are reviewing the routine for Homework later (5 min).

 STUDENTS TO LISTEN TO RECORDINGS WITH AN ENGLISH SPEAKER. TELL THEM TO STOP THE RECORDINGS IF THERE ARE ANY WORDS THEY DON'T UNDERSTAND FOR THE ENGLISH SPEAKER TO EXPLAIN (10 MIN).

Give Homework

 Give the students the Weekly Review Template and a copy of the pictures used in the lesson. Tell them to listen to their recordings and practice pointing to the correct pictures during the week. They should transcribe the recordings and try repeating what they hear. Remind them to bring the transcriptions to class for the next lesson for you to check for accuracy.

Riding a Bike

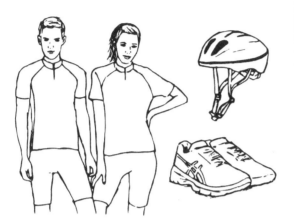

1. Wear riding clothing.

2. Find a flat location to ride, away from traffic.

3. Put on a helmet.

4. Adjust the bike seat.

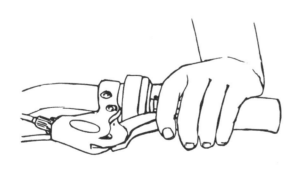

5. Test the brakes.

6. Start with one foot on the ground.

7 Start gliding. Push yourself off with your foot.

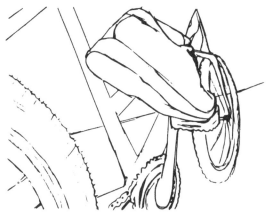

8 Start pedaling.

9 Look straight ahead.

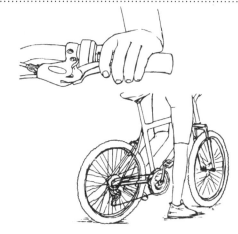

10 Dismount the bike. Stop pedaling and squeeze both handbrakes.

Give Homework

 LISTEN TO YOUR RECORDING OF THE TEACHER GIVING THE STEPS FOR RIDING A BIKE AND WRITE DOWN WHAT YOU HEAR.

Listen to the recording again and try repeating what you hear, sentence by sentence. See if you can also point to the correct pictures/perform the correct action as you repeat the recording. Remember to bring this to class with you next week!

....

....

....

....

Parking a Car

You will need
- Car (if possible)
- Weekly Review Template
- Smartphone

Review

Recap last week's lesson and check students' homework activities (10 min).

Parking a Car Routine

1. To park forwards, slowly steer the car in the direction of the parking spot Remember to lightly press the brake.

2. Pull into the parking space.

3. Press down on the brake.

4. Turn your wheels in the correct direction.

5. Shift the car into Park (P) and put the parking brake on.

6. To park backwards, shift the car into Reverse (R). Remember to lightly press the brake.

7. Steer your car in the direction of the parking spot.

8. Pull into the parking spot. Make sure you check your mirrors.

9. Press the brake firmly.

10. Shift to Park (P).

1. Ask the students "Who drives a car?" (5 min).

2. Go through the routine (10 min).

3. Go through the routine again quickly and this time have the students record it on their phones (5 min).

4. As a class, role play the process of parking a car. If possible, actually go through the routine with a real car (15 min).

5. Describe an aspect of the setting, such as the car, and have the students record the description on their phones, i.e. "The car has a steering wheel. On the ground are pedals for the accelerator and the brake. It also has a parking brake for when you are parked. There are mirrors so you can see out each side while you drive, etc." (5 min).

6. Have the students take a photo of the setting to remind them of it when they are reviewing the routine for Homework later (5 min).

STUDENTS TO LISTEN TO RECORDINGS WITH AN ENGLISH SPEAKER. TELL THEM TO STOP THE RECORDINGS IF THERE ARE ANY WORDS THEY DON'T UNDERSTAND FOR THE ENGLISH SPEAKER TO EXPLAIN (10 MIN).

Give Homework

Give the students the Weekly Review Template and a copy of the pictures used in the lesson. Tell them to listen to their recordings and practice pointing to the correct pictures during the week. They should transcribe the recordings and try repeating what they hear. Remind them to bring the transcriptions to class for the next lesson for you to check for accuracy.

 **ESL** # Parking a Car

1 To park forwards, slowly steer the car in the direction of the spot. Remember to lightly press the brake.

2 Pull into the parking space.

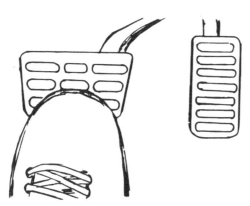

3 Press down on the brake.

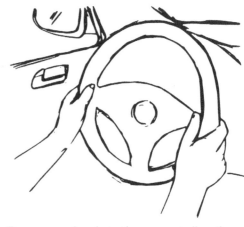

4 Turn your wheels in the correct direction.

5 Shift the car into Park (P) and put the parking brake on.

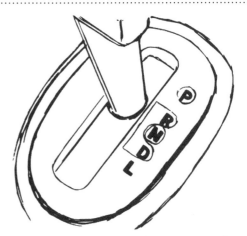

6 To park backwards, shift the car into Reverse (R). Remember to lightly press the brake.

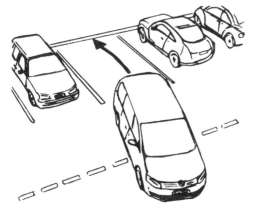

7 Steer your car in the direction of the parking spot.

8 Pull into the parking spot. Make sure you check your mirrors.

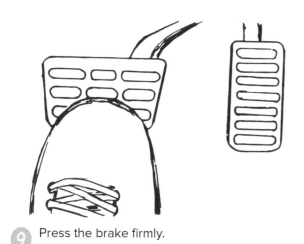

9 Press the brake firmly.

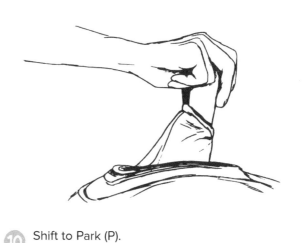

10 Shift to Park (P).

Give Homework

> LISTEN TO YOUR RECORDING OF THE TEACHER GIVING THE STEPS FOR PARKING A CAR AND WRITE DOWN WHAT YOU HEAR.

Listen to the recording again and try repeating what you hear, sentence by sentence. See if you can also point to the correct pictures/perform the correct action as you repeat the recording. Remember to bring this to class with you next week!

Getting a Driver's License

You will need
- Driver Guidebook (i.e. the driving rules book for the region you are in)
- Weekly Review Template
- Smartphone

Review

Recap last week's lesson and check students' homework activities (10 min).

Getting a Driver's License Routine

1. Study the driver's handbook for your local area (for example, in New South Wales, Australia it is called the Driver Knowledge Test Handbook).

2. Practice the test on your computer at home.

3. Book an appointment for your driving test.

4. Go to the service center where you booked your test.

5. Complete an application. You will need to bring documents that prove your identity.

6. Take an eyesight test.

7. Take your driving test. In NSW it is called the Driver Knowledge Test.

8. Find out the results of your tests.

9. If you passed, pay the testing and license fee.

10. Get your picture taken for your license.

   » Now you have a learner license. In NSW you can drive if someone who already has a license is watching you.

1. Ask the students "Who has a license and can drive?" (5 min).

2. Go through the routine (10 min).

3. Go through the routine again quickly and this time have the students record it on their phones (5 min).

4. Have the students roleplay the routine, including practicing a driving test. They may be able to attempt a practice test online using their phones.

5. Describe the service center and have the students record the description on their phones, i.e. "The transport office has eyesight charts on the wall. There are lots of chairs and computers. There are people standing behind the desks. They are wearing uniforms, etc." (5 min).

6. Have the students take a photo of the setting to remind them of it when they are reviewing the routine for Homework later (5 min).

STUDENTS TO LISTEN TO RECORDINGS WITH AN ENGLISH SPEAKER. TELL THEM TO STOP THE RECORDINGS IF THERE ARE ANY WORDS THEY DON'T UNDERSTAND FOR THE ENGLISH SPEAKER TO EXPLAIN (10 MIN).

Give Homework

Give the students the Weekly Review Template and a copy of the pictures used in the lesson. Tell them to listen to their recordings and practice pointing to the correct pictures during the week. They should transcribe the recordings and try repeating what they hear. Remind them to bring the transcriptions to class for the next lesson for you to check for accuracy.

Community Life ESL

Getting a Driver's License

1. Study the driver's handbook.

2. Practice the test on your computer at home.

3. Book an appointment for your driving test.

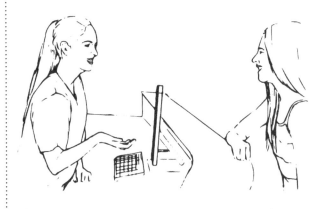

4. Go to the service centre where you booked your test.

5. Complete an application. You will need to bring documents that prove your identity.

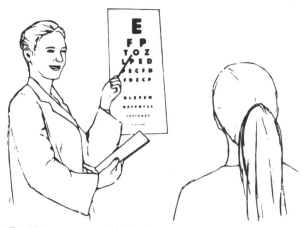

6. Take an eyesight test.

7 Take your driving test.

8 Find out the results of your test.

9 If you passed, pay the testing and license fee.

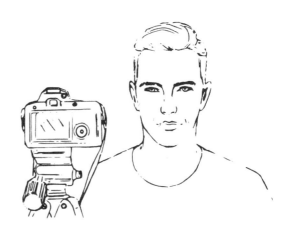

10 Get your picture taken for your license.

Give Homework

 LISTEN TO YOUR RECORDING OF THE TEACHER GIVING THE STEPS FOR GETTING A DRIVER'S LICENSE AND WRITE DOWN WHAT YOU HEAR.

Listen to the recording again and try repeating what you hear, sentence by sentence. See if you can also point to the correct pictures/perform the correct action as you repeat the recording. Remember to bring this to class with you next week!

....

....

....

....

Visiting the Doctor

You will need
- Weekly Review Template
- Smartphone

Review

Recap last week's lesson and check students' homework activities (10 min).

Going to the Doctor Routine

1. Search on the internet for local medical centers.

2. Choose one and go to the website.

3. Call the number.

4. Make an appointment, i.e. "Hi, my name is… and I would like to make an appointment to visit the doctor."

5. Ask for any details you need, i.e. "What time should I come? What is the address?"

6. Tell the receptionist you have arrived, i.e. "Hi, my name is…and I have an appointment."

7. Sit in the waiting room until your name is called.

8. Go with the doctor into the office

9. Tell the doctor your problem/symptoms, i.e. "My throat hurts…"

10. Follow the doctor's instructions, i.e. if he/she gives you a prescription, go to a pharmacy to get the medicine.

1. Ask the students "Which medical center do you go to?" or "What is going to the doctor like where you are from?"

2. Go through the routine (10 min).

3. Go through the routine again quickly and this time have the students record it on their phones (5 min).

4. Role play the routine as a class and have one student volunteer to do all the steps (10 min).

5. Have the students role play the routine with an English speaker, taking turns being the receptionist/doctor and the patient (10 min).

6. Describe the doctor's office and have the students record the description on their phones, i.e. "The doctor's office has two chairs and a desk. It has a bed in one corner. There are charts on the walls. The charts have pictures of the human body, etc." (5 min).

7. Have the students take a photo of the setting to remind them of it when they are reviewing the routine for Homework later (5 min).

 STUDENTS TO LISTEN TO RECORDINGS WITH AN ENGLISH SPEAKER. TELL THEM TO STOP THE RECORDINGS IF THERE ARE ANY WORDS THEY DON'T UNDERSTAND FOR THE ENGLISH SPEAKER TO EXPLAIN (10 MIN).

Give Homework

 Give the students the Weekly Review Template and a copy of the pictures used in the lesson. Tell them to listen to their recordings and practice pointing to the correct pictures during the week. They should transcribe the recordings and try repeating what they hear. Remind them to bring the transcriptions to class for the next lesson for you to check for accuracy.

Visiting the Doctor

1 Search on the internet for local medical centers.

2 Choose one and go to the website.

3 Call the number.

4 Make an appointment, i.e. "Hi, my name is… and I would like to make an appointment to visit the doctor.

5 Ask for any details you need, i.e. "What time should I come? What is the address?".

6 Tell the receptionist you have arrived, i.e. "Hi, my name is… and I have an apointment".

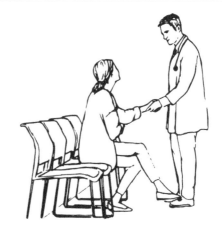

 Sit in the waiting room until your name is called.

Go with the doctor into the office.

Follow the doctor's instructions, i.e. if he/she gives you a prescription, go to a pharmacy to get the medicine.

 Tell the doctor your problem/symptoms, i.e. "My throat hurts...".

Give Homework

LISTEN TO YOUR RECORDING OF THE TEACHER GIVING THE STEPS FOR VISITING THE DOCTOR AND WRITE DOWN WHAT YOU HEAR.

Listen to the recording again and try repeating what you hear, sentence by sentence. See if you can also point to the correct pictures/perform the correct action as you repeat the recording. Remember to bring this to class with you next week!

....

....

....

....

Buying Medicine at the Pharmacy

You will need
- Prescription
- Medicine
- Weekly Review Template
- Smartphone

Review

Recap last week's lesson and check students' homework activities (10 min).

Buying Medicine at the Pharmacy Routine

1. Get a prescription at the doctor's office.

2. Go to the pharmacy.

3. Take your prescription to the prescription desk. There may be a sign that says, "Scripts In".

4. Give your prescription to the pharmacist.

5. Wait until they call your name. They may tell you to wait for a few minutes.

6. The pharmacist may give you instructions on how to take the medicine.

7. Get anything else you need from the pharmacy. The medicines on the shelves do not need a prescription and you can take them off the shelf.

8. Take your medicine to the front desk.

9. Pay for your medicine.

10. Take your medicine. Make sure to follow the pharmacist's instructions and the instructions on the medicine.

1. Ask the students "Have you bought medicine at the pharmacy? Is the pharmacy here the same as in your country or different?" (5 min).

2. Go through the routine (10 min).

3. Go through the routine again quickly and this time have the students record it on their phones (5 min).

4. As a class, role play the process of buying medicine at the pharmacy (15 min).

5. Describe an aspect of the setting, such as the pharmacy, and have the students record the description on their phones, i.e. "The pharmacy has a desk where you take your script. There are aisles with medicines on the shelves. There are staff ready to help you choose the right medicine. At the front is the checkout where you can pay for your medicine, etc." (5 min).

6. Have the students take a photo of the setting to remind them of it when they are reviewing the routine for Homework later (5 min).

 STUDENTS TO LISTEN TO RECORDINGS WITH AN ENGLISH SPEAKER. TELL THEM TO STOP THE RECORDINGS IF THERE ARE ANY WORDS THEY DON'T UNDERSTAND FOR THE ENGLISH SPEAKER TO EXPLAIN (10 MIN).

Give Homework

 Give the students the Weekly Review Template and a copy of the pictures used in the lesson. Tell them to listen to their recordings and practice pointing to the correct pictures during the week. They should transcribe the recordings and try repeating what they hear. Remind them to bring the transcriptions to class for the next lesson for you to check for accuracy.

Community Life ESL — Buying Medicine at the Pharmacy

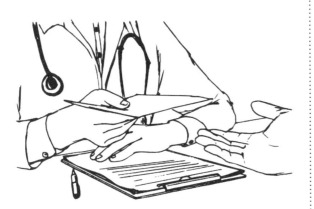

1 Get a prescription at the doctor's office.

2 Go to the pharmacy.

SCRIPTS IN

3 Take your prescription to the prescription desk. There may be a sign that says, "Scripts In".

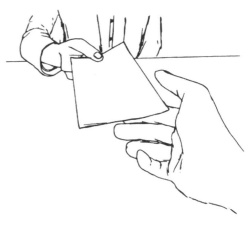

4 Give your prescription to the pharmacist.

5 Wait until they call your name. They may tell you to wait for a few minutes.

6 The pharmacist may give you instructions on how to take the medicine.

7 Get anything else you need from the pharmacy. The medicines on the shelves do not need a prescription and you can take them off the shelf.

8 Take your medicine to the front desk.

9 Pay for your medicine.

10 Take your medicine. Make sure to follow the pharmacist's instructions and the instructions on the medicine.

 ## Give Homework

 LISTEN TO YOUR RECORDING OF THE TEACHER GIVING THE STEPS FOR BUYING MEDICINE AT THE PHARMACY AND WRITE DOWN WHAT YOU HEAR.

Listen to the recording again and try repeating what you hear, sentence by sentence. See if you can also point to the correct pictures/perform the correct action as you repeat the recording. Remember to bring this to class with you next week!

Booking a Hotel

You will need
- Weekly Review Template
- Smartphone

Review

Recap last week's lesson and check students' homework activities (10 min).

Booking a Hotel Routine

1. Decide how much you want to pay, i.e. your budget.

2. Think about what type of accommodation you need, how many beds and bathrooms you will need, etc.

3. Think about your ideal holiday location.

4. Search for hotels online. Remember to include information like how many nights you need, the ideal location and any other specific things you want.

5. Compare hotels to find the best price.

6. Reserve the room online.

7. Pay for the room with your credit card.

8. Save the receipt.

9. Read over the receipt to make sure all the details are correct.

10. Call the hotel if you have any questions.

1. Ask the students "What are you planning to do in your holidays?" (5 min).

2. Go through the routine (10 min).

3. Go through the routine again quickly and this time have the students record it on their phones (5 min).

4. As a class, role play the process of booking a hotel (15 min).

5. Describe an aspect of the setting, such as the hotel website, and have the students record the description on their phones, i.e. "The website has lots of rooms to choose from. It has options for single and double rooms. It has a list of facilities, like a gym, restaurant, and spa. You can reserve the room on the website and pay with your credit card, etc." (5 min).

6. Have the students take a photo of the setting to remind them of it when they are reviewing the routine for Homework later (5 min).

 STUDENTS TO LISTEN TO RECORDINGS WITH AN ENGLISH SPEAKER. TELL THEM TO STOP THE RECORDINGS IF THERE ARE ANY WORDS THEY DON'T UNDERSTAND FOR THE ENGLISH SPEAKER TO EXPLAIN (10 MIN).

Give Homework

 Give the students the Weekly Review Template and a copy of the pictures used in the lesson. Tell them to listen to their recordings and practice pointing to the correct pictures during the week. They should transcribe the recordings and try repeating what they hear. Remind them to bring the transcriptions to class for the next lesson for you to check for accuracy.

Community Life ESL Booking a Hotel

① Decide on how much you want to pay, i.e. your budget.

② Think about what type of accommodation you need, how many beds and bathrooms you will want, etc.

③ Think about your ideal holiday location.

④ Search for hotels online. Remember to include information like how many nights you need, the ideal location and any other specific things you want.

⑤ Compare hotels to find the best price.

⑥ Reserve the room online.

7 Pay for the room with your credit card.

8 Save the receipt.

9 Read over the receipt to make sure all the details are correct.

10 Call the hotel if you have any questions.

📝 Homework

 LISTEN TO YOUR RECORDING OF THE TEACHER GIVING THE STEPS FOR BOOKING A HOTEL AND WRITE DOWN WHAT YOU HEAR.

Listen to the recording again and try repeating what you hear, sentence by sentence. See if you can also point to the correct pictures/perform the correct action as you repeat the recording. Remember to bring this to class with you next week!

Booking Flights

You will need
- Weekly Review Template
- Smartphone

Review

Recap last week's lesson and check students' homework activities (10 min).

Booking Flights Routine

1. Decide on your travel plans, like where you want to travel and how long you will be away, etc.

2. If you are flexible with your plans, you might get a better deal.

3. Search online to find the best flights.

4. Compare flights to find the best price.

5. Keep a list of the airfares.

6. When you have decided on your flight, purchase your ticket.

7. Pick your meal and seat preferences.

8. Provide your frequent flyer number and how many pieces of baggage you will have.

9. Print or save your booking confirmation.

10. Remember to take the booking confirmation and your passport with you to the airport.

1. Ask the students "Where would you like to fly on your next holiday?" (5 min).

2. Go through the routine (10 min).

3. Go through the routine again quickly and this time have the students record it on their phones (5 min).

4. As a class, role play the process of booking flights (15 min)

5. Describe an aspect of the setting, such as the plane, and have the students record the description on their phones, i.e. "The plane has aisles with seats. You can pick a window or aisle seat. There is a baggage compartment above the seat for your bags. The seats have seatbelts and arm rests. There is a bathroom at the end of the plane and also a place to get snacks and drinks, etc." (5 min).

6. Have the students take a photo of the setting to remind them of it when they are reviewing the routine for Homework later (5 min).

 STUDENTS TO LISTEN TO RECORDINGS WITH AN ENGLISH SPEAKER. TELL THEM TO STOP THE RECORDINGS IF THERE ARE ANY WORDS THEY DON'T UNDERSTAND FOR THE ENGLISH SPEAKER TO EXPLAIN (10 MIN).

Give Homework

 Give the students the Weekly Review Template and a copy of the pictures used in the lesson. Tell them to listen to their recordings and practice pointing to the correct pictures during the week. They should transcribe the recordings and try repeating what they hear. Remind them to bring the transcriptions to class for the next lesson for you to check for accuracy.

Community Life ESL Booking Flights

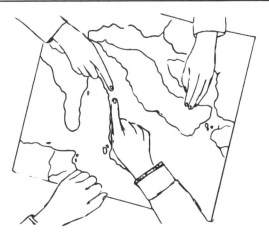

1. Decide on your travel plans, like where you want to travel and how long you will be away, etc.

2. If you are flexible with your plans, you might get a better deal.

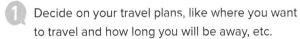

3. Search online to find the best flights.

4. Compare flights to find the best price.

5. Keep a list of the airfares.

6. When you have decided on your flight, purchase your ticket.

7 Pick your meal and seat preferences.

8 Provide your frequent flyer number and how many pieces of baggage you will have.

9 Print or save your booking confirmation.

10 Remember to take the booking confirmation and your passport with you to the airport.

 ## Homework

 LISTEN TO YOUR RECORDING OF THE TEACHER GIVING THE STEPS FOR BOOKING FLIGHTS AND WRITE DOWN WHAT YOU HEAR.

Listen to the recording again and try repeating what you hear, sentence by sentence. See if you can also point to the correct pictures/perform the correct action as you repeat the recording. Remember to bring this to class with you next week!

LEVEL 3 - INTERMEDIATE

Understanding a Story: Past, Present & Future

You will need

- English speakers ready to share their life story
- Weekly Review Template
- Smartphone

Review

Recap last week's lesson and check students' homework activities (10 min).

1. Talk about the importance of getting to know people deeply and understanding their life story.

   You might say the following: "In this class we want to help you make a lot of friends who speak English. It's good to get to know friends well so you know how they think and what is important to them. To do that, you need learn something about their life. This term you will talk with many different people and learn about what happened in their past and about their plans for the future. Be ready to ask a lot of questions!"

2. Talk about good questions that help to get to know someone well. As a class, come up with questions and write the list on the board (15 min).

Past: "Asking questions can help you get to know someone better. You can ask questions about things that happened in the past. Where are you from? What do you remember about your life growing up?" Have students come up with more questions.

Present: "You can ask questions about the present. How do you spend your time now? Can you tell me about your family?" Have students come up with more questions.

Future: "You can ask questions about the future. What will you do after this class? Will you go on any trips this year? What would you like to do that you aren't already doing?" Have students come up with more questions.

3. Have an English speaker share their life story (10 min). Model asking them questions from the list on the board from each of the categories (past, present and future).

 TELL STUDENTS TO RECORD THE STORY ON THEIR PHONES.

4. Have the students ask any follow up questions they have about the person's life that they can ask to finish (5 min).

"Sometimes when people tell you about their life, it leaves you with more questions. Does anyone have another question you want to ask about his/her life?"

Practice

Pair the students with English speakers and have the English speakers share their life story with the students. Remind the students to ask them questions from the list on the board (10 min).

 ## Give Homework

Give the students the Weekly Review Template. Tell them to listen to their recording of the story during the week. They should transcribe the recording and try repeating what they hear. Remind them to bring the transcription to class for the next lesson for you to check for accuracy.

Understanding Unusual Situations

You will need
- English speakers ready to share a story
- Weekly Review Template
- Smartphone

Review

Recap last week's lesson and check students' homework activities (10 min).

1. Talk about the importance of asking questions to get to know people better.

   "People like it when you ask them questions about their life. A good way to get to know someone better is to ask them about unusual situations in their life."

2. Have an English speaker share an unusual situation from their life (10 min).

 TELL STUDENTS TO RECORD THE STORY ON THEIR PHONES.

3. Come up with questions to ask about the unusual situation (10 min).

   "Today you will learn to ask questions about unusual things that happen in people's lives. Was there something that you thought was unusual about his/her story? Here are some examples of questions you could ask."

   » You said that you were stung by a stingray. What did you do?

   » You said when you were young you were fearful of being kidnapped by strangers. Did that ever happen? Tell us a little about that.

Have the students come up with more questions and write the list on the board.

4. Encourage the students to take turns asking the English speaker questions from the list on the board (5 min).

Practice

Pair the students with English speakers and have the English speakers share about something unusual that happened to them, i.e. something difficult or surprising, like a sudden illness, etc. Remind the students to ask follow-up questions (10 min).

 ## Give Homework

Give the students the Weekly Review Template. Tell them to listen to their recording of the story during the week. They should transcribe the recording and try repeating what they hear. Remind them to bring the transcription to class for the next lesson for you to check for accuracy.

Understanding Compared Experiences

You will need
- English speakers ready to share their story
- Weekly Review Template
- Smartphone

Review

Recap last week's lesson and check students' homework activities (10 min).

1. Talk about the importance of first listening and then speaking.

   "It is good to first listen to how an English person speaks and after that you can try to copy them. This will help you sound like a local person. "

   "When people tell you about something, they often compare things to help them describe it well. You will need to learn to compare things too when you speak."

2. Have an English speaker compare two events, places or experiences (15 min).

   TELL STUDENTS TO RECORD THE STORY ON THEIR PHONES.

3. Come up with questions to ask about the comparison (15 min).

   "Here are some examples of questions you could ask to get people to compare events."

   » You said that life is different today than it was when you were little. What has changed?

   » You said that you once lived in a small village for two months. Was life better or worse than here? What did you like about it? What did you not like about it?

   Have the students come up with more questions and write the list on the board.

4. Encourage the students to take turns asking the English speaker questions from the list on the board (5 min).

Practice

Pair the students with English speakers and have the English speakers compare two holidays they remember, a good one and a bad one. Remind the students to ask follow-up questions (10 min).

 ## Give Homework

Give the students the Weekly Review Template. Tell them to listen to their recording of the story during the week. They should transcribe the recording and try repeating what they hear. Remind them to bring the transcription to class for the next lesson for you to check for accuracy.

Retelling a Life Story

You will need
- English speakers ready to share their life story
- Weekly Review Template
- Smartphone

Review

Recap last week's lesson and check students' homework activities (10 min).

1. Talk about the importance of retelling stories.

   "Retelling a story helps you learn to tell stories like a local person. Today we will listen to a story about someone's life and then you can try to retell the story."

2. Have an English speaker briefly share an overview of their life story, including their future plans (5 min).

 TELL STUDENTS TO RECORD THE STORY ON THEIR PHONES.

3. As a class, write a brief overview of the main points of the story (15 min).

   "What are some things you remember about their life?" Help students come up with a basic overview of the life story and write bullet points on the board.

4. Have the students take turns retelling part of the life story (10 min).

5. Have the English speaker remind the students of things they have forgotten or retell any parts of the story where the students made mistakes.

Practice

Pair the students with English speakers and have the English speakers share a brief overview of their life story. Encourage the students to try retelling the story. Remind the English speakers to make any corrections as needed (10 min).

Give Homework

Give the students the Weekly Review Template. Tell them to listen to their recording of the story during the week. They should transcribe the recording and try repeating what they hear. Remind them to bring the transcription to class for the next lesson for you to check for accuracy.

Retelling an Unusual Experience

You will need
- English speakers ready to share a story
- Weekly Review Template
- Smartphone

Review

Recap last week's lesson and check students' homework activities (10 min).

1. Introduce the topic for the lesson.

   "Today you will learn to retell a story that someone has told about an unusual experience. It could be something that was exciting, memorable or life changing. Or it could be something that took someone by surprise. We all have unusual things that happen in our lives that make us different from other people."

2. Have an English speaker share about an unusual experience from their life (5 min).

 TELL STUDENTS TO RECORD THE STORY ON THEIR PHONES.

3. As a class, write a brief overview of the main points of the story (15 min).

   "Think about what he/she told us about the unusual situation. What made it unusual? What happened? How did he/she handle the situation?" Help students come up with a basic overview of the unusual situation and write bullet points on the board.

4. Have a student volunteer to retell the story (10 min).

5. Have the English speaker remind the student of things they have forgotten or retell any parts of the story where the student made mistakes.

Practice

Pair the students with English speakers and have the English speakers share about an unusual situation from their life, e.g. something that happened in their childhood. Encourage the students to try retelling the story. Remind the English speakers to make any corrections as needed (10 min).

 ## Give Homework

Give the students the Weekly Review Template. Tell them to listen to their recording of the story during the week. They should transcribe the recording and try repeating what they hear. Remind them to bring the transcription to class for the next lesson for you to check for accuracy.

Retelling Compared Events

You will need
- English speakers ready to share a story
- Weekly Review Template
- Smartphone

Review

Recap last week's lesson and check students' homework activities (10 min).

1. Introduce the topic for the lesson.

   "Today you will listen to someone compare events and then you can try to retell the story the way they did."

2. Have an English speaker briefly compare two events, experiences or places (5 min).

 TELL STUDENTS TO RECORD THE STORY ON THEIR PHONES.

3. As a class, write a brief overview of the main points of the story (15 min).

   "Think about what he/she told us about the events. How was it the same? How was it different?" Help the students come up with a basic overview of the unusual situation and write bullet points on the board.

4. Have a student volunteer to retell the story (10 min).

5. Have the English speaker remind the student of things they have forgotten or retell any parts of the story where the student made mistakes.

Practice

Pair the students with English speakers and have the English speakers compare two activities, i.e. a favorite activity and an activity they dislike. Encourage the students to try retelling the story. Remind the English speakers to make any corrections as needed (10 min).

Give Homework

Give the students the Weekly Review Template. Tell them to listen to their recording of the story during the week. They should transcribe the recording and try repeating what they hear. Remind them to bring the transcription to class for the next lesson for you to check for accuracy.

Sharing Your Story

You will need
- Weekly Review Template
- Smartphone

Review

Recap last week's lesson and check students' homework activities (10 min).

1. Talk about the importance of sharing your life story.

    "It's good to get to know your friends' life stories. But it is also important for them to get to know your story. This will help them understand you better and the things that are important to you."

2. As a class, come up with a list of things that are important to include in a life story and write the list on the board (10 min).

Past: Where are you from? Where were you born? What are some of the most important events in your life so far?

Present: How do you spend your time now? Can you describe your family?

Future: Do you have any big plans for the future? Will you go on any trips this year? What would you like to do that you aren't already doing?

3. Have a student volunteer to share their life story with the class (10 min). The students can ask them questions from the list on the board from each of the categories if they need prompting (past, present and future).

4. Have the students ask any follow up questions they have about the person's life that they can ask to finish.

    "Sometimes when people tell you about their life, it leaves you with more questions. Does anyone have another question you want to ask about his/her life?"

Practice

Pair the students with English speakers and have the students share their life story. The English speakers can ask them questions from the board if they need prompting (20 min).

"Now you get to tell the story of your own life. Think about what you'd like to say about your life story and future plans. Talk about where you were born and where you are from. Tell a story from your life growing up. Tell the story of your life till now. Describe your family. Explain what you do now and what your daily life is like today and your plans for the future."

ONCE THE STUDENTS HAVE TOLD THEIR STORY, HAVE THE ENGLISH SPEAKERS TRY RETELLING THE STORY FOR THE STUDENTS TO RECORD AS AN EXAMPLE TO LISTEN TO LATER.

 ## Give Homework

Give the students the Weekly Review Template. Tell them to listen to their recording of the story during the week. They should transcribe the recording and try repeating what they hear. Remind them to bring the transcription to class for the next lesson for you to check for accuracy.

Sharing an Unusual Experience

You will need
- Weekly Review Template
- Smartphone

Review

Recap last week's lesson and check students' homework activities (10 min).

1. Introduce the topic for the lesson.

   Today you will learn to talk about an unusual situation from your life.

2. As a class, come up with a list of things that are important to include when sharing about unusual situations and write the list on the board (10 min).

   "What made it unusual? What happened? How did you handle the situation?" Write bullet points on the board.

3. Have a student volunteer to share about an unusual situation that happened to them with the class (10 min).

4. Have the class ask any follow up questions they have about unusual experience that they can ask to finish.

   "Sometimes when people tell an unusual or surprising story, it leaves you with more questions. Does anyone have another question you want to ask him/her?"

Practice

Pair the students with English speakers and have the student share about an unusual experience that happened to them, e.g. something exciting or memorable like moving countries, having a baby, etc. The English speakers can ask them questions from the board if they need prompting (20 min).

   "Now it is your turn to tell about something unusual that happened in your life. It could be something exciting or life changing. Maybe it was something that took you by surprise. We all have unusual things that happen in our lives that are different from other people."

ONCE THE STUDENTS HAVE TOLD THEIR STORY, HAVE THE ENGLISH SPEAKERS TRY RETELLING THE STORY FOR THE STUDENTS TO RECORD AS AN EXAMPLE TO LISTEN TO LATER.

 ## Give Homework

Give the students the Weekly Review Template. Tell them to listen to their recording of the story during the week. They should transcribe the recording and try repeating what they hear. Remind them to bring the transcription to class for the next lesson for you to check for accuracy.

Comparing Events

You will need
- Weekly Review Template
- Smartphone

Review

Recap last week's lesson and check students' homework activities (10 min).

1. Introduce the topic for the lesson.

   "Today you will learn to compare two events, experiences or places."

2. As a class, come up with a list of things that are important to include when comparing experiences and write the list on the board (10 min).

   "How is it the same? How is it different? Which one is better?" Write the bullet points on the board.

3. Have a student volunteer to compare two events with the class (10 min). The students can ask them questions from the list on the board.

4. Have students ask any follow up questions they have about the person's life that they can ask to finish.

   "Sometimes when people tell you about something, it leaves you with more questions. Does anyone have another question you want to ask what he/she described?"

Practice

Pair the students with English speakers and have the students compare two places, e.g. their home country and the country they now live in. The English speakers can ask them questions from the board if they need prompting (20 min).

"Now you get to compare your life experience to the experience of those around you. Think about one example of how your life experience is the same as those around you, and one example of how your life experience is different. Start by explaining where you are from. Mention some ways life is the same in that place and some ways it is different."

ONCE THE STUDENTS HAVE TOLD THEIR STORY, HAVE THE ENGLISH SPEAKERS TRY RETELLING THE STORY FOR THE STUDENTS TO RECORD AS AN EXAMPLE TO LISTEN TO LATER.

Give Homework

Give the students the Weekly Review Template. Tell them to listen to their recording of the story during the week. They should transcribe the recording and try repeating what they hear. Remind them to bring the transcription to class for the next lesson for you to check for accuracy.

LEVEL 4 - INTERMEDIATE

Attitudes towards Change

You will need
- Weekly Review Template
- Smartphone

Review

Recap last week's lesson and check students' homework activities (10 min).

1. Talk about the importance of learning others' opinions and being able to share your own opinion in order to make deep friendships.

    "In this class you will learn how to make deeper friendships. This means you will need to learn about people's beliefs and motivations in life so you can talk about the life issues they are going through. What is important to them? What do they believe? You will also need to share your opinions and give reasons why you hold those beliefs."

2. Talk about good questions to ask to start discussing a topic (10 min).

    "This term you will learn to talk about lots of topics that are important to people. This will help you get to know your friends better and it will also help your friends get to know you better too.

    There are lots of questions you can ask to get to know what your friends believe about a topic."

    Benefits and Difficulties: *You can ask about the benefits and difficulties of this topic. What are the good things they see? What problems do they see?*

    Conflicting Opinions: *You can ask questions that show the opposite of their opinion. Some people say this. But what do they think?*

    Solutions: *You can ask about what would help avoid the difficulties and add to the benefits. What advice would they give?*

    Unfamiliar Contexts: *You can ask about unfamiliar contexts that your friends know about. Do they know of other places where things are the same?*

3. Introduce the topic for the class (5 min).

   "Our topic for today is change. What do people believe about change? Is it a good thing? You will get to ask the English speakers what that think. But first, let's come up with some questions that you can ask."

4. As a class, come up with a list of questions that could be asked about the topic. Think of questions for each category on the board (10 min).

   Benefits and Difficulties: *You can ask about the benefits and difficulties of a topic. Is outside influence and change a good thing? What kinds of problems do they see? What are some of the greatest difficulties that come with change?*

   Conflicting Opinions: *You can ask questions that show the opposite of their opinion. Some people say change helps you stay relevant. But others think it can be harmful and disruptive. What would they say to someone who thinks that way?*

   Solutions: *You can ask about what would help avoid the difficulties and add to the benefits. What advice would they give to children and adults in this area?*

   Unfamiliar Contexts: *You can ask about unfamiliar contexts that your friends know about. Do they know of other places where change has affected the community?*

5. Have a brief conversation with an English speaker on the topic of change. Model asking them questions from the list on the board from each of the categories (5 min).

 TELL STUDENTS TO RECORD THE STORY ON THEIR PHONES.

Practice

Pair the students with English speakers and encourage them to have a conversation on the topic of change. Remind the students to ask them questions from the list on the board (10 min).

Give Homework

Remind the students to listen to their recording of the conversation during the week. They should make notes on any important thoughts or questions they have. They should bring this to class for the next lesson.

Encourage the students to have a conversation during the week on the topic of change with a friend who speaks English.

Individual vs. Group Actions

You will need
- Weekly Review Template
- Smartphone

Review

Recap last week's lesson and check students' homework activities (10 min).

1. Introduce the topic for the class (5 min).

   "Our topic for today is individual versus group actions and decisions. You may have noticed that some people like working together and some people prefer working on their own. Some people like competing and want to win, others just want to have fun together and don't care who wins.

   In some countries people like to do things in groups. In others, people like to do things on their own. Understanding more about individual and group actions will help you act in normal ways. Remember, becoming a typical member of a community takes time- so be patient! Can you think of some examples of group and individual activities?"

2. As a class, come up with a list of questions that could be asked about the topic. Think of questions for each category on the board (15 min).

   "There are many questions you can ask to get to know what your friends believe about individual and group actions and decisions."

   Benefits and Difficulties: *You can ask about the benefits and difficulties of this topic. What are some of the benefits or difficulties when people act individually? What are the benefits or difficulties from cooperating? What are the reasons for this?*

   Conflicting Opinions: *You can ask questions that show the opposite of their opinion. Some people say it would be easier to decide things for themselves and not worry what the group thinks. What do they say to this idea?*

   Solutions: *You can ask about what would help avoid the difficulties and add to the benefits. What kinds of competition are ok? What should be done in groups and what should be done individually? What advice would they give to children and adults in this area?*

Unfamiliar Contexts: You can ask about unfamiliar contexts that your friends know about. Do they know of other places where people think differently about individual and group actions?

3. Have a brief conversation with an English speaker on the topic of individual vs. group actions. Model asking them questions from the list on the board from each of the categories (10 min).

 TELL STUDENTS TO RECORD THE STORY ON THEIR PHONES.

Practice

Pair the students with English speakers and encourage them to have a conversation on the topic of individual vs. group actions. Remind the students to ask them questions from the list on the board (10 min).

 ## Give Homework

Remind the students to listen to their recording of the conversation during the week. They should make notes on any important thoughts or questions they have. They should bring this to class for the next lesson.

Encourage the students to have a conversation during the week on the topic of individuality with a friend who speaks English.

Shameful vs. Praise-worthy Behavior

You will need
- Weekly Review Template
- Smartphone

Review

Recap last week's lesson and check students' homework activities (10 min).

1. Introduce the topic for the class (5 min).

   "Our topic for today is shameful behavior and behavior to be proud of. Perhaps you have noticed that some people do things in the community that others are ashamed of. What kinds of behavior are people really proud of? Can you think of some examples?"

2. Share an example with the class from your own experience or the community that illustrates this point. For example, maybe you know someone who crashed their car after drinking and driving? Or maybe you heard of someone in the community who saved someone from drowning at the beach?

3. As a class, come up with a list of questions that could be asked about the topic. Think of questions for each category on the board (15 min).

   "There are many questions you can ask to get to know what your friends believe about shameful behavior and behavior to be proud of. "

   Benefits and Difficulties: *You can ask about the benefits and difficulties of this topic. What are the biggest problems with shameful behavior? What is considered shameful? What is considered behavior to be proud of?*

   Conflicting Opinions: *You can ask questions that show the opposite of their opinion. For example, some people say that yelling in public is actually ok. What would they say about that?*

   Solutions: *You can ask about what might help avoid the difficulties and add to the benefits. For shameful behavior, is there anything that can be done so it happens less? What kinds of people could be good examples for others in the way they behave?*

Unfamiliar Contexts: You can ask about some unfamiliar contexts that your friends and neighbors know about. Do they know of other places where these behaviors are thought of differently?

4. Have a brief conversation with an English speaker on the topic of shameful behavior and behavior to be proud of. Model asking them questions from the list on the board from each of the categories (10 min).

 TELL STUDENTS TO RECORD THE STORY ON THEIR PHONES.

Practice

Pair the students with English speakers and encourage them to have a conversation on the topic of shamful behavior and behavior to be proud of. Remind the students to ask them questions from the list on the board (10 min).

 Give Homework

Remind the students to listen to their recording of the conversation during the week. They should make notes on any important thoughts or questions they have. They should bring this to class for the next lesson.

Encourage the students to have a conversation during the week on the topic of shame and pride with a friend who speaks English.

Roles and Responsibilities

You will need
- Weekly Review Template
- Smartphone

Review

Recap last week's lesson and check students' homework activities (10 min).

1. Introduce the topic for the class (5 min).

    "Our topic for today is the roles and responsibilities of different members of the community. For example, perhaps you have noticed that men do certain jobs and women do others. Or perhaps young people have certain jobs and so do children. Can you think of some examples?"

2. Share an example with the class from your own experience or the community that illustrates this point. For example, maybe you have worked somewhere where your colleagues were all the same gender? Or maybe you heard of someone in the community who does a job that is normally only done by young people?

3. As a class, come up with a list of questions that could be asked about the topic. Think of questions for each category on the board (15 min).

    "There are many questions you can ask to get to know what your friends believe about roles and responsibilities."

    Benefits and Difficulties: *You can ask about the benefits and difficulties of this topic. What is hard about being a man or woman or child in this community? What are some advantages?*

    Conflicting Opinions: *You can ask questions that show the opposite of their opinion. For example, some people say that children should work more and play less. What would they say about that?*

    Solutions: *You can ask about what would help avoid the difficulties and add to the benefits. What can be done to make sure people fulfil their roles in the community? What advice would they give to traditional people in this area?*

Unfamiliar Contexts: You can ask about unfamiliar contexts that your friends know about. Do they know of other places where people have different roles and responsibilities?

4. Have a brief conversation with an English speaker on the topic of roles and responsibilities. Model asking them questions from the list on the board from each of the categories (10 min).

 TELL STUDENTS TO RECORD THE STORY ON THEIR PHONES.

Practice

Pair the students with English speakers and encourage them to have a conversation on the topic of roles and responsibilities. Remind the students to ask them questions from the list on the board (10 min).

 Give Homework

Remind the students to listen to their recording of the conversation during the week. They should make notes on any important thoughts or questions they have. They should bring this to class for the next lesson.

Encourage the students to have a conversation during the week on the topic of responsibilities with a friend who speaks English.

Ways to Disagree and Reconcile

You will need
- Weekly Review Template
- Smartphone

Review

Recap last week's lesson and check students' homework activities (10 min).

1. Introduce the topic for the class (5 min).

   "Our topic for today is ways to disagree, and ways to reconcile when you have offended someone. For example, perhaps you have noticed that at times people in the community disagree. This happens with adults, young people and children as well. Can you think of some examples?"

2. Share an example with the class from your own experience or the community that illustrates this point. For example, maybe there is a current debate in the community on a certain topic? Or maybe someone in your family isn't speaking to another family member?

3. As a class, come up with a list of questions that could be asked about the topic. Think of questions for each category on the board (15 min).

   "There are many questions you can ask to get to know what your friends believe about ways to disagree and reconcile."

   Benefits and Difficulties: *You can ask about the benefits and difficulties of this topic. What are the biggest difficulties that come with conflict? Are there any benefits that come from times of conflict?*

   Conflicting Opinions: *You can ask questions that show the opposite of their opinion. For example, some people say that friendships between children are difficult because children always fight, and so children should be kept apart. What would they say about that?*

   Solutions: *You can ask about what would help avoid the difficulties and add to the benefits. What can be done to avoid conflicts? What advice would they give to adults, young people and children in this area?*

Unfamiliar Contexts: You can ask about unfamiliar contexts that they know about. Do they know of other places where people handle conflict differently?

4. Have a brief conversation with an English speaker on the topic of ways to disagree and reconcile. Model asking them questions from the list on the board from each of the categories (10 min).

 TELL STUDENTS TO RECORD THE STORY ON THEIR PHONES.

Practice

Pair the students with English speaker and encourage them to have a conversation on the topic of ways to disagree and reconcile. Remind students to ask them questions from the list on the board (10 min).

 ## Give Homework

Remind the students to listen to their recording of the conversation during the week. They should make notes on any important thoughts or questions they have. They should bring this to class for the next lesson.

Encourage the students to have a conversation during the week on the topic of disagreement with a friend who speaks English.

Successful vs. Unsuccessful People

You will need
- Weekly Review Template
- Smartphone

Review

Recap last week's lesson and check students' homework activities (10 min).

1. Introduce the topic for the class (5 min).

    "Our topic for today is successful and unsuccessful people in the community and why people think of them like that. For example, perhaps you have noticed that some people are viewed as more successful than others. Why are they considered successful? Can you think of some examples?"

2. Share an example with the class from your own experience or the community that illustrates this point. For example, maybe there is someone in the community who is successful, and people are envious of them? Maybe you know someone who is considered unsuccessful and people think of them negatively?

3. As a class, come up with a list of questions that could be asked about the topic. Think of questions for each category on the board (15 min).

    "There are many questions you can ask to get to know what your friends believe about successful and unsuccessful people."

    Benefits and Difficulties: *You can ask about the benefits and difficulties of this topic. What are the main benefits of being successful? What are the main difficulties?*

    Conflicting Opinions: *You can ask questions that show the opposite of their opinion. Perhaps some people say that success only brings trouble and bad attitudes on both sides. What would they say about that?*

    Solutions: *You can ask about what would help avoid the difficulties and add to the benefits. How should successful people behave towards others? What people are good and bad examples of this?*

    Unfamiliar Contexts: *You can ask about unfamiliar contexts that they know about. Do they know of other places where people have different ideas of being successful and unsuccessful?*

4. Have a brief conversation with an English speaker on the topic of successful and unsuccessful people. Model asking them questions from the list on the board from each of the categories (10 min).

 TELL STUDENTS TO RECORD THE STORY ON THEIR PHONES.

Practice

Pair the students with English speakers and encourage them to have a conversation on the topic of successful and unsuccessful people. Remind students to ask them questions from the list on the board (10 min).

 ## Give Homework

Remind the students to listen to their recording of the conversation during the week. They should make notes on any important thoughts or questions they have. They should bring this to class for the next lesson.

Encourage the students to have a conversation during the week on the topic of success with a friend who speaks English.

Personal vs. Public Space

You will need
- Weekly Review Template
- Smartphone

Review

Recap last week's lesson and check students' homework activities (10 min).

1. Introduce the topic for the class (5 min).

   "Our topic for today is opinions people have about personal and public space. For example, perhaps you have noticed that when people talk to one another, they don't sit very close or make eye contact often. Or maybe people are welcome to come and talk in people's front gardens, but they don't normally go into the house. Can you think of some examples?"

2. Share an example with the class from your own experience or the community that illustrates this point. For example, maybe children are expected to sit separately to adults at your family gatherings? Maybe there are some places in the community that are open to visit anytime, and some that are closed to others?

3. As a class, come up with a list of questions that could be asked about the topic. Think of questions for each category on the board (15 min).

   "There are many questions you can ask to get to know what your friends believe about personal and public space."

   Benefits and Difficulties: *You can ask about the benefits and difficulties of this topic. What are ways of marking space? What are the main benefits or difficulties of this?*

   Conflicting Opinions: *You can ask questions that show the opposite of their opinion. Perhaps some people say that property and space boundaries don't need to be respected. What do they think about that?*

   Solutions: *You can ask about what would help avoid the difficulties and add to the benefits. What advice would they give to adults, young people and children in this area? What people are good examples of this?*

   Unfamiliar Contexts: *You can ask about unfamiliar contexts that they know about. Do they of other places where people have different ideas of personal and public space?*

4. Have a brief conversation with an English speaker on the topic of personal and public space. Model asking them questions from the list on the board from each of the categories (10 min).

 TELL STUDENTS TO RECORD THE STORY ON THEIR PHONES.

Practice

Pair the students with English speakers and encourage them to have a conversation on the topic of personal and public space. Remind the students to ask them questions from the list on the board (10 min).

 Give Homework

Remind the students to listen to their recording of the conversation during the week. They should make notes on any important thoughts or questions they have. They should bring this to class for the next lesson.

Encourage the students to have a conversation during the week on the topic of personal and public space with a friend who speaks English.

Rules for Visiting

You will need
- Weekly Review Template
- Smartphone

Review

Recap last week's lesson and check students' homework activities (10 min).

1. Introduce the topic for the class (5 min).

    "Our topic for today is having visitors and the rules for visiting others. For example, perhaps you have noticed that people often visit each other at night after they finish work. When they visit, they talk about sport or their plans for holidays or the weekend. What are some rules for visiting that you know about?"

2. Share an example with the class from your own experience or the community that illustrates this point. For example, maybe your family often invites friends along to the park for barbeques on the weekend. Perhaps everyone who comes is expected to bring food along to share?

3. As a class, come up with a list of questions that could be asked about the topic. Think of questions for each category on the board (15 min).

    "There are many questions you can ask to get to know what your friends believe about having visitors and rules for visiting."

    Benefits and Difficulties: *You can ask about the benefits and difficulties of this topic. What are the main benefits and difficulties of visiting others? What are common reasons why people visit?*

    Conflicting Opinions: *You can ask questions that show the opposite of their opinion. Perhaps some people say that visiting isn't important. What do they think about that?*

    Solutions: *You can ask about what would help avoid the difficulties and add to the benefits. How should people care for visitors? What advice would they give to adults, young people and children in this area? What people are good and bad examples of this?*

Unfamiliar Contexts: *You can ask about unfamiliar contexts that they know about. Do they know of other places where people have different rules for visiting?*

4. Have a brief conversation with an English speaker on the topic of rules for visiting. Model asking them questions from the list on the board from each of the categories (10 min).

 TELL STUDENTS TO RECORD THE STORY ON THEIR PHONES.

Practice

Pair the students with English speakers and encourage them to have a conversation on the topic of rules for visiting. Remind students to ask them questions from the list on the board (10 min).

 ## Give Homework

Remind the students to listen to their recording of the conversation during the week. They should make notes on any important thoughts or questions they have. They should bring this to class for the next lesson.

Encourage the students to have a conversation during the week on the topic of rules for visiting with a friend who speaks English.

Peace vs. Fear

You will need
- Weekly Review Template
- Smartphone

Review

Recap last week's lesson and check students' homework activities (10 min).

1. Introduce the topic for the class (5 min).

   "Our topic for today is peace and fear in the community. For example, perhaps you have noticed that people seek things in order to feel secure and at peace in the community. Maybe having a good job or lots of friends is important to them. On the other hand, perhaps you've noticed that some things really bring fear. This might be sickness, death or being poor. Can you think of other examples?"

2. Share an example with the class from your own experience or the community that illustrates this point. For example, maybe you know someone who works for the government and everyone wants to be their friend because they are hoping to get something from them? Perhaps your friends are all trying to get a good job because rent and house prices are so high?

3. As a class, come up with a list of questions that could be asked about the topic. Think of questions for each category on the board (15 min).

   "There are many questions you can ask to get to know what your friends believe about peace and fear."

   Benefits and Difficulties: *You can ask about the benefits and difficulties of this topic. What things bring peace and security? What things bring fear and insecurity? What are the benefits and difficulties of those things?*

   Conflicting Opinions: *You can ask questions that show the opposite of their opinion. Perhaps some people say jobs and education aren't important for peace and security. What do they think about that?*

   Solutions: *You can ask about what would help avoid the difficulties and add to the benefits. What would they like to change so they have less fear and insecurity? What advice would they give to adults, young people and children in this area? What does a good example of peace and security look like?*

Unfamiliar Contexts: You can ask about unfamiliar contexts that they know about. Do they know of other places where people have different ideas of what brings peace and fear?

4. Have a brief conversation with an English speaker on the topic of peace and fear. Model asking them questions from the list on the board from each of the categories (10 min).

 TELL STUDENTS TO RECORD THE STORY ON THEIR PHONES.

Practice

Pair the students with English speakers and encourage them to have a conversation on the topic of peace and fear. Remind students to ask them questions from the list on the board (10 min).

 Give Homework

Remind the students to listen to their recording of the conversation during the week. They should make notes on any important thoughts or questions they have. They should bring this to class for the next lesson.

Encourage the students to have a conversation during the week on the topic of peace and fear with a friend who speaks English.

Making Goals

You will need
- Weekly Review Template
- Smartphone

Review

Recap last week's lesson and check students' homework activities (10 min).

1. Introduce the topic for the class (5 min).

   "Our topic for today is making goals. What kind of goals do people in the community make? For example, perhaps you have noticed that some people are trying to save money to buy a house. Or maybe you have noticed that others work long hours so they can support family members. Can you think of other examples of goals people make?"

2. Share an example with the class from your own experience or the community that illustrates this point. For example, maybe you know someone who started their own business and is trying to 'get ahead' that way? Or perhaps your family say that education is important in order to be respected in the community?

3. As a class, come up with a list of questions that could be asked about the topic. Think of questions for each category on the board (15 min).

   "There are many questions you can ask to get to know what your friends believe about making goals."

   Benefits and Difficulties: *You can ask about the benefits and difficulties of this topic. What are the benefits and difficulties of making long-term goals?*

   Conflicting Opinions: *You can ask questions that show the opposite of their opinion. Perhaps some people say making goals is not a good idea. Different people have different goals. Perhaps some people say that lending money to friends and family is more important than saving it. What do they think about that?*

   Solutions: *You can ask about what would help avoid the difficulties and add to the benefits. What are their long-term goals? What advice would they give to adults, young people and children in this area? What is a bad example of a person pursuing long-term goals?*

Unfamiliar Contexts: You can ask about unfamiliar contexts that they know about. Do they know of other places where people make different goals?

4. Have a brief conversation with an English speaker on the topic of making goals. Model asking them questions from the list on the board from each of the categories (10 min).

 TELL STUDENTS TO RECORD THE STORY ON THEIR PHONES.

Practice

Pair the students with English speakers and encourage them to have a conversation on the topic of making goals. Remind students to ask them questions from the list on the board (10 min).

 ## Give Homework

Remind the students to listen to their recording of the conversation during the week. They should make notes on any important thoughts or questions they have. They should bring this to class for the next lesson.

Encourage the students to have a conversation during the week on the topic of making goals with a friend who speaks English.

Showing Affection

You will need
- Weekly Review Template
- Smartphone

Review

Recap last week's lesson and check students' homework activities (10 min).

1. Introduce the topic for the class (5 min).

   "Our topic for today is ways to show affection. How do people in the community demonstrate affection and what kinds of physical contact are ok? Perhaps you have noticed that people show affection in certain ways at different ages. For example, perhaps people like to hold babies and children, especially mothers. Can you think of some examples of ways to show affection?"

2. Share an example with the class from your own experience or the community that illustrates this point. For example, maybe it's normal for husbands and wives to sit together and hug and kiss in public? Or perhaps the men you know don't normally show physical affection to each other?

3. As a class, come up with a list of questions that could be asked about the topic. Think of questions for each category on the board (15 min).

   "There are many questions you can ask to get to know what your friends believe about the appropriate ways to show affection."

   Benefits and Difficulties: *You can ask about the benefits and difficulties of a topic. What is the proper way to greet people for the first time? What are the benefits and difficulties with showing affection and physical contact?*

   Conflicting Opinions: *You can ask questions that show the opposite of their opinion. Perhaps some people say that showing affection in public only leads to problems. What do they think about that?*

   Solutions: *You can ask about what would help avoid the difficulties and add to the benefits. What advice would they give to adults, young people and children in this area? What does a good example of showing affection look like?*

Unfamiliar Contexts: *You can ask about unfamiliar contexts that they know about. Do they know of other places where people show affection differently?*

4. Have a brief conversation with an English speaker on the topic of showing affection. Model asking them questions from the list on the board from each of the categories (10 min).

TELL STUDENTS TO RECORD THE STORY ON THEIR PHONES.

Practice

Pair students with English speakers and encourage them to have a conversation on the topic of showing affection. Remind the students to ask them questions from the list on the board (10 min).

 ## Give Homework

Remind the students to listen to their recording of the conversation during the week. They should make notes on any important thoughts or questions they have. They should bring this to class for the next lesson.

Encourage the students to have a conversation during the week on the topic of showing affection with a friend who speaks English.

Family Life

You will need
- Weekly Review Template
- Smartphone

Review

Recap last week's lesson and check students' homework activities (10 min).

1. Introduce the topic for the class (5 min).

    "Our topic for today is family life. What is the definition of family and what are normal family rules? Perhaps you have noticed that people think of a family as only a husband, wife and children, or is it bigger than that? What are the responsibilities of family members towards each other?"

2. Share an example with the class from your own experience or the community that illustrates this point. For example, maybe it's normal for parents to discipline children, but not anyone else? Maybe most of your friends tend to space and plan children when growing their family?

3. As a class, come up with a list of questions that could be asked about the topic. Think of questions for each category on the board (15 min).

    "There are many questions you can ask to get to know what your friends believe about the family life and rules."

    Benefits and Difficulties: *You can ask about the benefits and difficulties of this topic. What are the benefits and difficulties of being part of a family? What are the benefits and difficulties of disciplining children, or planning well for their future?*

    Conflicting Opinions: *You can ask questions that show the opposite of their opinion. Perhaps some people say that the small family unit isn't as important as extended family. What do they think about that?*

    Solutions: *You can ask about what would help avoid the difficulties and add to the benefits. What advice would they give to adults, young people and children in this area? What does a good and bad example of a family look like?*

    Unfamiliar Contexts: *You can ask about unfamiliar contexts that they know about. Do they know of other places where people think differently about family life?*

4. Have a brief conversation with an English speaker on the topic of family life. Model asking them questions from the list on the board from each of the categories (10 min).

 TELL STUDENTS TO RECORD THE STORY ON THEIR PHONES.

Practice

Pair the students with English speakers and encourage them to have a conversation on the topic of family life. Remind students to ask them questions from the list on the board (10 min).

 ## Give Homework

Remind the students to listen to their recording of the conversation during the week. They should make notes on any important thoughts or questions they have. They should bring this to class for the next lesson.

Encourage the students to have a conversation during the week on the topic of family life with a friend who speaks English.

Dating and Marriage

You will need
- Weekly Review Template
- Smartphone

Review

Recap last week's lesson and check students' homework activities (10 min).

1. Introduce the topic for the class (5 min).

    "Our topic for today is dating and marriage. How does marriage come about? What is the process for dating?"

2. Share an example with the class from your own experience or the community that illustrates this point. For example, maybe people you know believe you should date multiple people before deciding on a marriage partner. Or perhaps your parents' marriage broke down and they got divorced?

3. As a class, come up with a list of questions that could be asked about the topic. Think of questions for each category on the board (20 min).

    "There are many questions you can ask to get to know what your friends believe about dating and marriage."

    Benefits and Difficulties: *You can ask about the benefits and difficulties of this topic. What are the benefits and difficulties with marriage? What are the difficulties and benefits of dating?*

    Conflicting Opinions: *You can ask questions that show the opposite of their opinion. Perhaps some people say cheating on your husband or wife isn't good, but it happens a lot and is just to be expected. What do they think about that?*

    Solutions: *You can ask about what would help avoid the difficulties and add to the benefits. What advice would they give to adults, young people and children in this area? What does a good and bad example of dating look like?*

    Unfamiliar Contexts: *You can ask about unfamiliar contexts that they know about. Do they know of other places where people think differently about dating and marriage?*

4. Have a brief conversation with an English speaker on the topic of dating and marriage. Model asking them questions from the list on the board from each of the categories (10 min).

 TELL STUDENTS TO RECORD THE STORY ON THEIR PHONES.

Practice

Pair the students with English speakers and encourage them to have a conversation of the topic of dating and marriage. Remind students to ask them questions from the list on the board (10 min).

 ## Give Homework

Remind the students to listen to their recording of the conversation during the week. They should make notes on any important thoughts or questions they have. They should bring this to class for the next lesson.

Encourage the students to have a conversation during the week on the topic of dating and marriage with a friend who speaks English.

Sickness and Death

You will need
- Weekly Review Template
- Smartphone

Review

Recap last week's lesson and check students' homework activities (10 min).

1. Introduce the topic for the class (5 min).

   "Our topic for today is sickness and death and its effect on people. What are the main reasons why people get sick? How do people deal with death?"

2. Share an example with the class from your own experience or the community that illustrates this point. For example, maybe you were involved in planning a funeral for a family member? You could talk about common traditions to do with burial practice.

3. As a class, come up with a list of questions that could be asked about the topic. Think of questions for each category on the board (15 min).

   "There are many questions you can ask to get to know what your friends believe about sickness and death."

   Benefits and Difficulties: *You can ask about the benefits and difficulties of this topic. Are there any benefits at all to sickness and death? What are the difficulties of sickness and death for those who are left behind, like widows and orphans?*

   Conflicting Opinions: *You can ask questions that show the opposite of their opinion. Perhaps some people say the cause of sickness is spiritual in nature. Or that people should see a spiritual healer, and not take medicine. What do they think about that?*

   Solutions: *You can ask about what would help avoid the difficulties and add to the benefits. What could people do to avoid getting sick? What advice would they give to adults, young people and children in this area?*

   Unfamiliar Contexts: *You can ask about unfamiliar contexts that they know about. Do they know of other places where people think differently about sickness and death?*

4. Have a brief conversation with an English speaker on the topic of sickness and death. Model asking them questions from the list on the board from each of the categories (10 min).

 TELL STUDENTS TO RECORD THE STORY ON THEIR PHONES.

Practice

Pair the students with English speakers and encourage them to have a conversation on the topic of sickness and death. Remind students to ask them questions from the list on the board (10 min).

 ## Give Homework

Remind the students to listen to their recording of the conversation during the week. They should make notes on any important thoughts or questions they have. They should bring this to class for the next lesson.

Encourage the students to have a conversation during the week on the topic of sickness and death with a friend who speaks English.

Government Rules

You will need
- Weekly Review Template
- Smartphone

Review

Recap last week's lesson and check students' homework activities (10 min).

1. Introduce the topic for the class (5 min).

   "Our topic for today is government rules and people's attitudes towards rule followers and rule breakers. How does the government give and enforce rules? What are some examples of government rules? How do people feel about the governments and its rules?"

2. Share an example with the class from your own experience or the community that illustrates this point. For example, maybe a new road rule is being enforced in the community? Maybe there are some rules that are ambiguous and open to interpretation?

3. As a class, come up with a list of questions that could be asked about the topic. Think of questions for each category on the board (15 min).

   "There are many questions you can ask to get to know what your friends believe about the government and its rules."

   Benefits and Difficulties: *You can ask about the benefits and difficulties of this topic. What are the benefits and difficulties of government influence and rules in the community?*

   Conflicting Opinions: *You can ask questions that show the opposite of their opinion. Perhaps some people say the police system is corrupt and unfair when offenses are committed. Or perhaps people say the government should be more involved in the community, especially in areas of health and education. What do they think about that?*

   Solutions: *You can ask about what would help avoid the difficulties and add to the benefits. Would they work in the government system if they had the opportunity? What advice would they give to adults, young people and children in this area? What does a good and bad example of government involvement look like?*

Unfamiliar Contexts: You can ask about unfamiliar contexts that they know about. Do they know of other places where people think differently about the government and its rules?

4. Have a brief conversation with an English speaker on the topic of the government and its rules. Model asking them questions from the list on the board from each of the categories (10 min).

 TELL STUDENTS TO RECORD THE STORY ON THEIR PHONES.

Practice

Pair the students with English speakers and encourage them to have a conversation on the topic of government rules. Remind students to ask them questions from the list on the board (10 min).

Give Homework

Remind the students to listen to their recording of the conversation during the week. They should make notes on any important thoughts or questions they have. They should bring this to class for the next lesson.

Encourage the students to have a conversation during the week on the topic of government rules with a friend who speaks English.

Beliefs about Spirits

You will need
- Weekly Review Template
- Smartphone

Review

Recap last week's lesson and check students' homework activities (10 min).

1. Introduce the topic for the class (5 min).

    "Our topic for today is spiritual beings. Do people in the community believe in spirits? How do people encounter them and interact with them?"

2. Share an example with the class from your own experience or the community that illustrates this point. For example, maybe there are people in the community who speak to dead people? Maybe other people you know believe that angels watch over them?

3. As a class, come up with a list of questions that could be asked about the topic. Think of questions for each category on the board (15 min).

    "There are many questions you can ask to get to know what your friends believe about spirits."

    Benefits and Difficulties: *You can ask about the benefits and difficulties of this topic. What are the benefits and difficulties of various spiritual beings?*

    Conflicting Opinions: *You can ask questions that show the opposite of their opinion. Perhaps some people say there are no such thing as spiritual beings. What do they think about that?*

    Solutions: *You can ask about what would help avoid the difficulties and add to the benefits. What can a person do to avoid difficultly with spiritual beings? What advice would they give to adults, young people and children in this area?*

    Unfamiliar Contexts: *You can ask about unfamiliar contexts that they know about. Do they know of other places where people think differently about spiritual beings?*

4. Have a brief conversation with an English speaker on the topic of spiritual beings. Model asking them questions from the list on the board from each of the categories (10 min).

 TELL STUDENTS TO RECORD THE STORY ON THEIR PHONES.

Practice

Pair the students with English speakers and encourage them to have a conversation on the topic of spiritual beings. Remind students to ask them questions from the list on the board (10 min).

 ## Give Homework

Remind the students to listen to their recording of the conversation during the week. They should make notes on any important thoughts or questions they have. They should bring this to class for the next lesson.

Encourage the students to have a conversation during the week on the topic of spiritual beings with a friend who speaks English.

Where History is Heading

You will need
- Weekly Review Template
- Smartphone

Review

Recap last week's lesson and check students' homework activities (10 min).

1. Introduce the topic for the class (5 min).

    "Our topic for today is where history and life are heading. Do people in the community believe that life goes in circles, or that it is heading somewhere? Is life getting better or worse? What do you think?"

2. Share an example with the class from your own experience or the community that illustrates this point. For example, maybe you feel that things were better in the community when you were young? Maybe people you know believe they will come back physically after they die?

3. As a class, come up with a list of questions that could be asked about the topic. Think of questions for each category on the board (15 min).

    "There are many questions you can ask to get to know what your friends believe about where history and life are heading."

    Benefits and Difficulties: *You can ask about the benefits and difficulties of this topic. How are time and history a benefit to a community? What are the difficulties that come when we try to control our lives and destinations?*

    Conflicting Opinions: *You can ask questions that show the opposite of their opinion. Perhaps some people say that no matter what you do on earth, you cannot change what happens to you after you die. Or perhaps people say that people should live how they want and not worry about history or life after death? What do they think about that?*

    Solutions: *You can ask about what would help avoid the difficulties and add to the benefits. What advice would they give to adults, young people and children in this area?*

Unfamiliar Contexts: You can ask about unfamiliar contexts that they know about. Do they know of other places where people think differently about where history and life are heading?

4. Have a brief conversation with an English speaker on the topic of where history and life are heading. Model asking them questions from the list on the board from each of the categories (10 min).

 TELL STUDENTS TO RECORD THE STORY ON THEIR PHONES.

Practice

Pair the students with English speakers and encourage them to have a conversation on the topic of where history and life are heading. Remind students to ask them questions from the list on the board (10 min).

 ## Give Homework

Remind the students to listen to their recording of the conversation during the week. They should make notes on any important thoughts or questions they have. They should bring this to class for the next lesson.

Encourage the students to have a conversation during the week on the topic of where history and life are heading with a friend who speaks English.

How the World Began

You will need
- Weekly Review Template
- Smartphone

Review

Recap last week's lesson and check students' homework activities (10 min).

1. Introduce the topic for the class (5 min).

   "Our topic for today is how the world began. What do people believe about how the world began? Was there anything that made this happen?"

2. Share an example with the class from your own experience or the community that illustrates this point. For example, maybe people you know believe the world evolved into what it is today without any spiritual beings involved in the process.

3. As a class, come up with a list of questions that could be asked about the topic. Think of questions for each category on the board (15 min).

   "There are many questions you can ask to get to know what your friends believe about how the world began."

   Benefits and Difficulties: *You can ask about the benefits and difficulties of this topic. How are the stories of origins a benefit or a difficulty to the community? Are the stories consistent and trustworthy?*

   Conflicting Opinions: *You can ask questions that show the opposite of their opinion. Perhaps some people say that spiritual beings did create the world, and so they should be respected. What do they think about that?*

   Solutions: *You can ask about what would help avoid the difficulties and add to the benefits. What advice would they give to adults, young people and children in this area?*

   Unfamiliar Contexts: *You can ask about unfamiliar contexts that they know about. Do they know of other places where people think differently about how the world began?*

4. Have a brief conversation with an English speaker on the topic of how the world began. Model asking them questions from the list on the board from each of the categories (10 min).

 TELL STUDENTS TO RECORD THE STORY ON THEIR PHONES.

Practice

Pair the students with English speakers and encourage them to have a conversation on the topic of how the world began. Remind students to ask them questions from the list on the board (10 min).

 ## Give Homework

Remind the students to listen to their recording of the conversation during the week. They should make notes on any important thoughts or questions they have. They should bring this to class for the next lesson.

Encourage the students to have a conversation during the week on the topic of how the world began with a friend who speaks English.

APPENDIX

Introduction to English Class

If possible, translate this paper into the students' languages before giving out.

This is our English class. We will be learning English each week.

This class is for learners who are spending time with local people and joining in activities that happen around them- not for those who only want to learn in a classroom.

Goals

At first, you will just listen. But soon you will start to speak.

There are many things you can do when you can speak English. You can get a job, make friends, speak on the phone, read signs and help your children with their schoolwork.

This class will help you make friends. You will learn how to speak, listen and act in ways that are normal in your community. You will learn how people think and what is important to them.

Homework

The more you practice, the faster you will learn. We will give you Homework Activities so you can practice at home and wherever you go.

Each week you will make a plan to learn English during the week using your Homework Activities.

The Homework we give you will include things to do that will help you get to know people and join in the things that they are doing. It is your job to spend lots of time with people. Things might not work out exactly as you planned. But it's good to start with a plan.

Plan

Make a plan that will help you spend as much time as possible in learning to speak, as well as spending time looking after your family and in your job. The more time you spend speaking, the faster you will learn.

Try to use the things you have to do each day or the place you work as a time to learn. You can visit local families with your own family, cook or shop with a friend, listen to English language TV shows, and learn the 'local way' of doing things at home and at work.

Helper

Try to find a friend who can speak both your language and English. Then they can help you with your homework. You can also bring them along to English class so they can find out what you are learning.

Get Ready

Some things to bring with you to class:

> »   A smartphone that records video and sound

> »   A notebook and pen

Getting Settled

Maybe you have recently moved to this country. As you get to know the people who live near you, watch the way they act and speak. Here are some things you can do:

> »   Watch the people around you, the places they go, and the things they do every day and ask them questions.

> »   Ask for help from local people as you settle in with housing, furniture, shopping, cooking, schools and so on. Be happy to ask for help. Let people help you when you need it most.

> »   Be friendly and let people get to know you and try to get to know them. Invite people into your home and go to their home when you are invited.

> »   Talk to neighbors, work colleagues, shopkeepers and your children's teachers.

At first, you will feel like there is a lot to learn. But that's ok, you can't learn everything at once! The best thing is to get to know the people around you as soon as you can. So spend as much time as you can where people usually spend most of their time- like the shops or park- and get to know these places first.

Learning English can be fun! Remember, you can ask us for help anytime and tell us what things you would like to learn to do and say.

Placement Test

Administer this short test to determine which level students should be placed in (either Levels 1 and 2, or Levels 3 and 4). The test should be done one-on-one and should take no more than ten to fifteen minutes with each student. It focuses on the student's level of comprehension and speaking, rather than their reading and writing proficiency.

The questions get progressively more difficult, so stop whenever you feel the student has reached the limit of their ability.

Level 1 and 2 (Beginner) - Able to complete up to question 4.

Level 3 and 4 (Intermediate) - Able to go beyond question 4.

You will need

- A page with pictures of 10 common objects (common animals, fruits and vegetables, numbers, etc.)

- A page with pictures of 10 common objects (colours, common household objects, vehicles, etc.)

1. Casual opening conversation:

   Hello, how are you today?

   (Continue with a short conversation as you are able)

   We are going to do a short test to see which English class will be the best one for you to join.

   Are you ready to begin?

   ☐ ABLE TO RESPOND TO MOST QUESTIONS WITH EASE

2. Listen and point:

   Show the student a page with pictures of ten common objects (common animals, fruits and vegetables, numbers, etc.).

   Say to the student: *Point to the (object).*

   Have the student listen and point to each object on the page as you ask them to point to each one.

   You should always say the name of the object in a simple sentence rather than on its own, e.g., *Where is the (object)? Show me the (object).*

   You can repeat this exercise with different picture pages.

   ☐ ABLE TO NAME MOST OBJECTS WITH EASE

3. Point and Name:

   Show the student a page with pictures of ten common objects (colors, common household objects, vehicles, etc.)

   Point to each object and say to the person: *What is this?*

   Have them name as many of the objects as they can.

   You can repeat this exercise with different picture pages.

   ☐ ABLE TO NAME MOST OBJECTS WITH EASE

4. Simple questions:

   Ask the student some simple questions to allow them to demonstrate their level of comprehension and speaking.

   What is your name? _____

   Where do you live? _____

   How many children do you have? _____

   How long have you been in this country? _____

   What is your job? _____

   Where do you work? _____

   What hobbies do you have? _____

   What do you enjoy doing on the weekend? _____

   Where would you like to travel? _____

   Extra question/s_____

   ☐ ABLE TO RESPOND TO MOST QUESTIONS WITH EASE

5. Comprehension exercise:

   Give the student the following story printed out. You should read the story out loud, and they can follow along reading it if they are able.

   Verbally ask them the questions about the story, and if they are able, they can read the questions as well. Have them answer the questions verbally.

   Bill has a young son named Sam. Sam loves to go to the park. The park is not far from their house. Sam and Bill play with a ball at the park. Bill kicks the ball, and Sam chases it. Sam is a fast runner. He kicks the ball back to Bill. Bill and Sam enjoy spending time together. Bill loves his son.

   1. Who is Sam?

   2. Where does Sam love to go?

   3. What do Sam and Bill do at the park?

   4. Where is the park?

   5. How does Bill feel about Sam?

   ☐ ABLE TO RESPOND TO MOST QUESTIONS WITH EASE

Recommended Starting Level: _____

Able to complete up to question 4= Recommended Starting Level 1

Able to go beyond question 4= Recommended Starting Level 3

Weekly Review

☐ Listen to your recordings for the lesson (for Levels 1 and 2 you can also try pointing to the correct pictures/performing the correct action/routine).

☐ As you listen, try repeating what you hear.

☐ Write down what you hear and ask a friend who speaks English if there are any words you don't understand. Remember to bring this to class with you for the next lesson!

Community Activity Template

1. Plan to observe a common routine in the community	Activity:
2. Participate in the routine with a friend. Try to join in if you can!	Friend:
3. List the routine steps *Remember to take photos of each step. Later you will use this when you have to do the routine yourself.	Steps:
4. Describe the setting	Description:

5. Ask a friend WHAT, WHERE, HOW, WITH WHAT, WHEN, and WHO questions: (i.e. How do I get to the pharmacy? Or Where is the pharmacy?)	Questions:
6. Note new words for objects/actions or any questions you have.	New Words/Further Questions:

Community Activity Ideas

Using Public Transport

Washing Dishes

Washing Clothes

Brushing Teeth

Grocery Shopping

Shopping for Clothes

Using an ATM

Borrowing from the Library

Making a Local Meal

Getting a Haircut

Going on a Bush Walk

Going to the Beach

Playing a Local Game

Attending a Local Sports Game

Attending a Church Service

Attending a Bible Study

Going to the Movies

Feeding or Bathing a Pet

Cooking a BBQ

Packing a School Lunch Box

Mowing the Grass

Potting a Plant

Ordering Pizza

Riding a Bike

Parking a Car

Washing a car

Visiting the Doctor

Buying Medicine at the Pharmacy

Choosing and Booking Flights/ Transportation

Choosing and Booking a Hotel

CPSIA information can be obtained
at www.ICGtesting.com
Printed in the USA
LVHW072157200321
681908LV00033B/442